Collected Poems 1952–83

Alan Brownjohn

By the same author

Poems
The Railings
The Lions' Mouths
Sandgrains on a Tray
Warrior's Career
A Song of Good Life
A Night in the Gazebo

For Children
To Clear the River (*as John Berrington*)
Brownjohn's Beasts

As Editor
First I Say This
New Poems 1970–71 (with Seamus Heaney and Jon Stallworthy)
New Poetry 3 (with Maureen Duffy)

Criticism
Philip Larkin

Collected Poems 1952–83

Alan Brownjohn

2330

Secker & Warburg · London

First published in England 1983 by
Martin Secker & Warburg Limited
54 Poland Street, London W1V 3DF

Copyright © Alan Brownjohn 1983

British Library Cataloguing in Publication Data

Brownjohn, Alan
  Collected poems 1952–83
  I. Title
  821'.914   PR6052.R62

  ISBN 0-436-07115-0

Printed in Great Britain by
Redwood Burn Ltd, Trowbridge

For my family and friends

Foreword

These two hundred poems come from six books, and from uncollected work done since the latest of them, *A Night in the Gazebo*, appeared in 1980. The other five books are *The Railings* (1961), which included certain poems from a very early booklet, *Travellers Alone* (1954), *The Lions' Mouths* (1967), *Sandgrains on a Tray* (1969), *Warrior's Career* (1972) and *A Song of Good Life* (1975). Notes appended to some of the poems in those volumes may be consulted there; they have been omitted from this collection. A selection of my work up to 1969 appeared in *Penguin Modern Poets 14*.

I have seen the received wisdom about collected editions change a lot during my writing lifetime. Some years ago it was thought desirable to prune published volumes severely when assembling a 'Collected', and revise (sometimes also rearrange) individual poems in a drastic way. But revisions made with an assumed wisdom of hindsight (the mature writer improving on the younger one) came in for much justified criticism. So the pendulum swung back. It was later thought better to put into a collected edition every, or nearly every, poem published in book form, without revisions, and to stand by them.

This collection follows a modified version of this second, I think more honest, procedure. A number of poems to be found in the six separate volumes have indeed gone: those which looked too slight or too occasional for inclusion, or echoed the themes and tones of others. But a few poems which tempted me to drop them for different reasons – because they now seemed peculiar, even alien – I have kept, in case what troubles the 'mature' self about such poems is in fact some kind of idiosyncratic life. And except for the correction of one or two factual errors, and the amendment of a couple of titles, no poem has been altered in any way at all.

The poems are arranged in the chronological order of their completion (thus changing the order in which they appeared in four out of the six books), but allocated here to the decades in which they were written. One tends to think more and more in decades towards the end of a century. The sequence 'A Song of Good Life', a set of twenty-one separate yet interconnecting poems finished together, is here given consecutive numbers.

January 1983   *Alan Brownjohn*

Contents

1970s
105–185

1950s

1 *The Animals*

Cutting the different shapes of bush,
He chances suddenly on the animal form:
Each shrub becomes a dog, a cat, a tiger.

Yet he does not stop to think as he crops
That in grief of leaf and branch they lack
The adequate life, that their roots
Bind them too sadly to possessive earth.

So he sleeps as the day declines, does not see
Their shadows yearn and lengthen,
And wistful, stretch in desire to be gone,
Away from the ordered garden, on legs
That cannot carry them, in living game.

And they grow as paradoxes, to be seen
Alive but still, sly, abject, posturing,
On the unmoving lawn – unchanged until
Their outlines fade with the growth of summer's
    green.

2 *The Train*

The train will come tomorrow year,
The signals clamber into signs,
The gates will open on the track
Where weeds have grown among the lines.

A murmur in the listening air
Besides the heart's emphatic beat
Will rise beyond the junction bridge
Out of the summer's static heat,

And round the distant, anxious bend
Engine and carriages appear.
But on a sultry afternoon
Your waiting hope could turn to fear.

Confronted with achieved desires
You may see nothing more to do
Than shrink from noise and turn away
As every devil thunders through.

3   *Travellers Alone*

Night in the streets we tired of
Hides daylight features in tangible dark,
Seals up, presents as finite, endlessness.
We shall not see the sequel to our journey
That every housetop valley spread for us,
Or suburbs' prospect of our wandering.
We shall forget the arriving trains, bound
For the town's heart from stations not our own.

Night hides it gently, cannot dare
The caught precision of the terraces
Shaped in their light of exposing summer,
Possesses cautious fears that will not trust
The corners to themselves, is guardian now
Of the clear river's dimmed façades,
Soothing with care the sharp path's angle
Into the square another statue marks.

Night is consoling, half-anaesthetic
To the full sense – till we see suddenly
The make of shadows friendly to the touch
Rebuke our confidence, the single lamps
Fade from their source, the windows close
Their watching, yellow eyes; then walls dissolve
Into the dark of any barren night,
Night not our friend, bereaved of human light.

4   A Garden in Summer

August is skilful in erasing fear,
And out of the full greenhouse into sunlight
I have now followed mine down the terraces
To find nothing where shore and garden meet.

On a clear sea's day it has no place,
Vanished, or simplified in the slanting light
Or under the mild oaks' shadows that turn
From shade to dusk. No place, that is, until

The absence of dread, pure sense of bondage broken, is itself
The burden feared, the freedom threatened suddenly.
And in a consciousness of joy the fear returns,
Fear that its wholeness must be too complete, its passing

Begin where even now the trees are still,
The air grows cold, a summer's tide drains out,
Horizons approach with the closeness of cloud,
And the slow warm wind through the garden falters, dies.

5 Fantasy

Fantasy means a landscape disturbed
By one dissimilar element – a chair
Moved by no hand or reason in your room,
A letter never sent and yet received.

These changes make no sense
In the expected world. There is no adjusting
Them to it – rather the world must change
To fit new features, systems reorganize.

You must now imagine each separate object,
Obvious and logical, set in a different scheme.
Walk backwards in the street, get up at night,
Plant sunflowers in your bedroom, play with bricks,
Until the world is altered, as a lens
That, blurred, comes suddenly clear, shows actual
    shapes.

And the scene, in the saner, accustomed brain
Sets now for disturbance to begin again.

6 A Teacher of the Deaf

(for C.E.)

Her purpose is to mould words for them, wholly
Out of the ordinary sight of things, make meanings
To link and connect with objects, to effect communication.
And from their silent country they stretch out
Their wordless thought to her indicating lips, they grasp
Aspects of movement in her face, and make them
Symbols for things themselves, in their feeling sense.

An object is the easiest. Think of *cat*,
The living animal that is, and moves;
(*Is*, of course, is a difficult word; existence
Is no simple attribute.) Yet, incidentally,
Think can be, surprisingly, quite quickly taught.
Thinking, somehow, can be told, or shown, or mimed –
A hand at the head, an expression, then an action.

But only slowly come the classes of things –
So easily confused with the things themselves.
Three cats will not mean *animal* in kind, but only *cats*.
And numbers, though they grasp them, do not help here;
They do not define, but merely multiply *cat*.
Or adjectives will be mistaken for what they describe:
Black cat seems *cat*, a *heavy* book – just *book*.

Yet these are the foothills of her mountain.
On steeper slopes come *for* and *to* and *the*,
. Articles, and prepositions of place. These are confused
With the actions done in teaching them. For example,
I walk to the door: walk and *door* are easily learnt,
But *to* and *the* slip by. Her patient lips
Convey a movement, but no meaning stirs.

Some means must be found and used, by way of signs,
To create the elusive sense of such expressions,
That the climbers might move on from the seen and known,
   and
Up to the strange, invisible *idea*. She will have to make actions
Seem to possess a meaning beyond the facts
And subtler than the movement. She will have to come
At last to the hardest in the range of word and thought,

The unseen abstract, content of mind alone.
This is an escarpment for her. What is *real*? *Unreal*?
Or what is *wise*? Or *foolish*? *Good*? Or *bad*?
But once beyond that, the mountain can be viewed
From its highest point; and her sense can be comprehended.
She has now to begin to point out the extended land,
For they, with this summit reached, can *understand*.

7 Moles

Beneath our feet (their silence calm as ours)
The unseen creatures laying waste this land
Wreck all the field we walk on, turning up
Their mounds of sun-bleached earth on every hand.

And yet their limit is the outer road
Which halts their upward progress at the hedge,
And on that lower ground their tunnels cease,
In watery daylight, at the river's edge.

Likewise, I doubt the power of any love
To wreck us further with its burrowing toil;
Now it has worked through our two narrow fields,
It finds no larger acres left to spoil.

Our minor beings are not wide enough
To let great love rear hills on their estate.
Their scope includes the gesture and the sigh,
But not the fire to leave them desolate.

8 11.30

If we are still together, it is because
Of the need to weed the garden.

Sustaining and disinterested deeds
(Which you might call love)
Are at a discount, but the house still stands.

Necessity does all this: if we are to eat
We need to wash some plates.

Turn the tap on for me, then (let
The water be hot!)

The hate and the unease will die in time
With the death-rattle of the draining sink.

9   *Scrutiny*

Hard as you scan yourself,
There is something that covers up
The person neglecting work,
The glutton and the bore,
The wholly unsociable half:

Replacing them with all
The qualities you prefer:
To be firm but compassionate,
Intolerant of cant,
Or constructively sceptical.

A self-deception which eases
The pestering shames away
Can be dangerous to have,
Can censor important faults,
Gloss over deserved disgraces

– But is mostly for the best:
What crippling horror would not,
Without it, invade the heart,
What doubt to shake the hand,
What guilt, destroying rest?

10 *By Daytime*

(for K.S.T.)

That one we speak of who would harm the sense
If we lay out in her by night and slept,
Is certainly tamed now; has nothing on
The uncomplicated sun;

Has by day no power
Quite equal to the beam which there
Distinguishes the sharp lake from the trees,
And clearly colours the heather
We do not gather.

She inhabits absentmindedly a sky
Not at all her own, ill-fitted to invoke
Her customary presences, and tides;

Seems almost of not much importance any more,
Though we should be fair
To her drained face,
Should admit that it has not been

A day or a place or a mood to worry out
A just opinion of the moon.

11 *Sin of Omission*

The window somewhere that I did not close,
Far back in the day's large hours,
Stands open still; and now at night
The deep house stirs, the corridors
Cold in the blank draught edging from room
     to room.
Where was the fault that has so surely let
Chance take its certain vengeance on the lazy;
Made curtains restless, distant doors uneasy?

This mere neglect, by daytime small, achieves
A shaming size by night. I listen
To the night's wind
And worry to decide if gracious sleep
Will intervene among the quartering chimes;
Or if I should get up and search about
And coldly grope to trace it in the dark
(The error I have made so many times)?

12 *Balance*

The ceremonious dispositions of hands
In the hushed air of blessing, in prayer,
In particular moments of love,

Contain the exactest peace. Their calm preserves
A dedicated poise: each holy act
Quietly instinct with deep restraint and tact.

They know they must not falter and betray
What is behind their skill. Their wisdom serves
To hold them back from gestures not in tune.

9

And so, for a short time, they do not tumble
Down from the ceremonious to the true:
They hover still; just manage not to show

That blessing very often condescends,
And prayer pleads up from self-wrought misery,
And love's hands can reach after loveless ends.

13 Facing Outwards

A garden pillar, where a grey stone lion
Stares with intended anger, always forward
Down between two plain lines of sheltering trees;
This I look at, and walk towards it now,
Some family symbol, cracked with rain and age
And tame through summer's branches; keeping but
A small part of the thing it stood to mark,
The mere pretence to a resounding rage.

Sometimes, indeed, the setting helps it out.
The winter sky has seagulls, vagrant-white,
Wheeling and crying over the bare trees.
And then the lion, on snow-lit afternoons,
Gains enough boldness just to look like some
Real beast perhaps, whose tawny dust has long
Vanished, like all the statue's dignity,
Blown about air down which the snow has come.

But most new seasons crown that head and trunk
With abject harmlessness; memorial to
A long-departed power, once making clear
The anger shown to strangers, and the pride;
Suddenly bringing back the period when
The vice inside them could not be made known
Except in terms of fearsome statuary,
Where it seemed virtuous in indignant stone.

The path trodden most goes confidently near
To the edge of the cliff; not even tufts of grass
Define a nominal boundary between
This hard mud track (for the easy walkers'
Steady shoes) and the drop.

Safely, some yards away, roams indistinctly
Another path: for the fearful and the cautious,
Running inside a fence put up for sheep.
Longer, but wiser, to go by this,
Though it gives no particular view of the sea.

If it has come to choosing here, then
Caution seems best. But look again, its path
Tangles through hedges and pools, and stops for
     stiles,
And nothing feels better now than the way
Which follows the dizzying parapet.

Walk that path. Surely no hurling gusts
Of today's bleak wind could unbalance you; no jut
Of risky earth would loosen to betray
Such daring feet; and haven't you nearly
Lost your old fear of heights?

15 *For a Journey*

House Field, Top Field, Oak Field, Third Field:
Though maps conclude their duties, the names trek on
Unseen across every county. Farmers call hillocks
And ponds and streams and lanes and rocks
By the first words to hand; a heavy, whittled-down
Simplicity meets the need, enough to help say
Where has yielded best, or the way they walked from
    home.

You can travel safely over land so named –
Where there is nowhere that could not somewhere
Be found in a memory which knows, and loves.
So watch then, all the more carefully, for
The point where the pattern ends: where mountains,
    even,
And swamps and forests and gaping bays acquire
The air of not needing ever to be spoken of.

Who knows what could become of you where
No one has understood the place with names?

16 *Lads*

At the next station climbed in
The Volunteers: 'Housman's Pride',
As the regiment might be called,
So full of 'love' and 'death',
Clean bombs and dirty songs.

The Old Irresponsibles,
With only themselves to keep
In cigarettes, drink and girls,
They scatter the silver paper
And bite the chocolate whole;

Then, shiftlessly sprawled and
          laughing,
In the uniform which makes
Them a no-man's-land between
Our peace and an actual war
They settle back to sleep.

17 A Day at Work

And through the parted curtains these grey cats
Came suddenly to sight. Turning their way,
He watched them while they roamed the floor between,
Then called some word or two, and made to rise;
But they had heard, and ran to meet this voice
With heads inclined and dim, obedient eyes.
Where he leant down they curled about his sleeve,
And still the storm howled on about the house;
Chilled with its lightning rooms where months of dust
Stood on the shelves, found the sure crack
Where hail could enter.
                    And his forgotten book
Lay open on the grass for rain to glance
Over each flurried page the wind blew back.

I watched the duration of the bubble.
Through seconds of my time it lived
Light-years of its own,
With the same reflected room on its luminous globe,
And down inside, a minute crimson world,
Intricately formed; as if to demonstrate how
The beautiful can sometimes be accidental.

Shaken into being from an obstinate pen,
It fell between the torn edge and the words
And stayed on the page (while I continued to write)
Unmoved by earthquakes of fingers and storms of
      breath;
A tiny dome, remaining propped above
Its floor of paper, stained with a dimmer red,
Until at last some unseen pressure broke

Glass wall, and wry, distended images,
And flattened the surface out.
It was as if it were wanting to repeat
That something will always weigh down upon beauty
Haphazardly built, that attempts to stand without
Foundations laid with thought for what they bear:
Beauty without effect except to mirror

Its creator for a time, then vanish, leaving
Scent or stain, only, of what had been there.

When it was Munich, I was eight.
Miss Adams made her point like this:
'Without a ruler, no one can
Draw me a line that's truly straight.'
And thus, to make her meaning plain:
'Not even any famous man:
Herr Hitler. Mr Chamberlain.'

And through the years, one might infer,
Miss Adams used such other names
As fitted best the days she came
To teach this truth, beloved of her:
'Not even Mr Stalin, and
Sir Winston Churchill, he's the same,
Could draw me one straight line freehand.'

And I should think that through that door,
In one of those brown passages,
I might still find her echoing room
Somewhere along the lower floor;
And hear again that doctrine taught,
To forty different minds for whom
It would seem just as strange a thought.

'No one who thinks that he can draw
Straight lines without a ruler, will
Ever surprise me if he fails –
What do you think your ruler's *for*?
There isn't anyone at all
Could do it. Not the Prince of Wales!
Not even General de Gaulle!'

As of some unproved right, the snow
Settles the outer suburbs now,
Laying its claim unhurriedly
On gnome and monkey-puzzle-tree.

Observe its power to shape and build,
Even in this unfruitful world,
Its white informal fantasies,
From roofs and paths and rockeries.

And swayed by such soft moods, I fall
Into forgiving nearly all
The aspirations of the place,
And what it does to save its face:

The calm and dutiful obsession
With what is 'best in our position',
The loyal and realistic views,
The rush-hours with the *Evening News* –

The snow fulfils its pure design
And softens every ugly line,
And for a while will exorcize
These virulent proprieties.

Within one mile of here there is
No lovelier place to walk than this,
On days when these kind flakes decide
That what it boasts of, they shall hide.

Because there is somebody washing below,
This tap rasps in its throat. I say again,
I should not really let my hands expect
Water at any time; yet despair must show
If this unnerving guttural cough has wrecked
My strenuous answer to the morning's rain.

The week has stopped at one cold point of day
By the empty bowl; the mirror holds and keeps,
For longer than it should, its uncombed image;
The razor which I hold must shave away
More parts of night; but at this arid stage,
Night seems to have returned, all action sleeps.

And time, it seems to me, now that I wait
Leaning in one white corner, crouched and still,
Means merely, What contains activity:
Those areas of waking which create
The sense of moving, doing, constantly,
However small the purpose they fulfil.

One unexpected pause in this will cheat
Time of such meaning as it can convey:
Minutes, deprived of their brief purposes,
Pass vacantly, no sign to indicate
You lived in every one of them: there is
No kind of time which these blank wastes obey.

If time's to work, it needs the tap to run,
And with its failure had this thought arrived:
In death, too, there may be no more than this,
No certain state of being lost or won
For world or silence—just some endless pause,
And into it, no message dropped to say,

Move to the next brief act which must be lived.

22 *Inheritance*

At seven in the damp light of morning I awoke
Uncomfortably into the room; to find
The windows then already steamed with heat.

A hand to the glass, I knew, would reveal at least
My nearest acres; and besides, that act
Would pass for something done, as surely as

Pens dipped in ink have nearly written words.
I would therefore wipe a gazing-space, a view,
As the day's beginning, token of tasks to come.

But with that gesture came a thing unguessed
In last night's darkness: quick, habitual weeds
Clustering every path, the trees deformed

By blight, or axes, and the fences left to fall.
I did not think this thrusting mockery
Would start so soon; yet knew I now must ask

How plan wide reason for this wide estate
With such needs close at hand? How think of miles
When each near yard fed such huge enemies?

23 *'In this city . . .'*

In this city, perhaps a street.
In this street, perhaps a house.
In this house, perhaps a room
And in this room a woman sitting,
Sitting in the darkness, sitting and crying
For someone who has just gone through the door
And who has just switched off the light
Forgetting she was there.

We are going to see the rabbit,
We are going to see the rabbit.
Which rabbit, people say?
Which rabbit, ask the children?
Which rabbit?
The only rabbit,
The only rabbit in England,
Sitting behind a barbed-wire fence
Under the floodlights, neon lights,
Sodium lights,
Nibbling grass
On the only patch of grass
In England, in England
(Except the grass by the hoardings
Which doesn't count.)
We are going to see the rabbit
And we must be there on time.

First we shall go by escalator,
Then we shall go by underground,
And then we shall go by motorway
And then by helicopterway,
And the last ten yards we shall have to go
On foot.

And now we are going
All the way to see the rabbit,
We are nearly there,
We are longing to see it,
And so is the crowd
Which is here in thousands
With mounted policemen
And big loudspeakers
And bands and banners,
And everyone has come a long way.

But soon we shall see it
Sitting and nibbling
The blades of grass
On the only patch of grass
In – but something has gone wrong!
Why is everyone so angry,
Why is everyone jostling
And slanging and complaining?

The rabbit has gone,
Yes, the rabbit has gone.
He has actually burrowed down into the earth
And made himself a warren, under the earth,
Despite all these people.
And what shall we do?
What *can* we do?

It is all a pity, you must be disappointed,
Go home and do something else for today,
Go home again, go home for today.
For you cannot hear the rabbit, under the earth,
Remarking rather sadly to himself, by himself,
As he rests in his warren, under the earth:
'It won't be long, they are bound to come,
They are bound to come and find me, even here.'

25 *William Empson at Aldermaston*

This is our dead sea, once a guidebook heath.
Left and right hands worked busily together
A parliament or two,
And there she stands:

Twelve miles of cooling pipes; concrete and secret
Warrens underground; clean little towers
Clamped with strong ladders; red, brisk vans
Which hurry round

The wide, kerbed avenues with pulsing lights
To signify danger; and all this
Extending still its miles, as seas possessed
Of power or anger

Will – except that here
The tide decrees, with threats in yellow paint,
Its own unquestioned bounds, keeps dogs to catch
Someone who gets

Beyond the fence: it seems that otherwise
We shiver from an unclean nakedness,
And need to clothe our hot emotions cold
With wire, and curs.

But let there be some praise, where that is due:
For paint, of enlivening colours, spent
On all these deathly offices. Where typists sit,
Who do not make the thing,

Or scientists, who do not fire the thing,
Or workers, who obey the scientists,
The rooms are beautiful. And anyone
Who passed by car one day

Not knowing what it was would never guess.
(Perhaps some urgent public undertaking
Set up for health, or water? Or a camp
Where other people went

On holidays?) Such airs of carnival,
With death designed as smiling, to conceal
His proper features – these things justified
Replies in kind:

An absurd fête of life, in one Friday field
For which no pass was needed. The effect:
Two sorts of carnival clashing: on this side
The mud, or grass,

The boots and stoves and caravans; that side,
The trim, discreet pavilions of the State.
And one more contrast marked these gaieties:
This side there seemed

Some thousands, while of death's there wasn't one.
Just the white-braided police returned the stare
Of the boys with haversacks, or the fierce
Empirical gaze

Of the man with the Chinese beard, or the pondering
    glance
Of the woman with the basket on wheels.
And some thought death's precise executives
Had told or asked

The servants of his will to stay away,
Hinting of jobs they might not like to lose,
And they had houses . . . from whose windows,
    next,
Many faces looked the way

Of the procession; speaking not a word,
But merely watching. How else, then, explain
If this was not the reason, why their children,
Through all the bands and singing,

All the beards and the guitars, did not come out;
But stood behind held curtains, listlessly,
With tight and puzzled faces, or peered through
Some furtive upstairs sunblind

While it passed? No coloured hat, not one
In all the range of shirts and slogans worn,
Seemed odder than these faces. That deep blankness
Was the real thing strange.

Except there are no graves or flowers,
He has made a miniature cemetery of his garden,
To advertise his stones. And every name

Hammered in granite in that tidy script
Is a scrupulous fiction: nobody I knew
Lived here with such a name; or ever, with it,

Married this wife he left so young and soon.
The first shock passing, which this skill
Appalled my eyes with, I walk on relieved,

Can almost smile. Yet the words presume a power
To be remembered longer than the names
Of strangers, read in passing, on real graves

At actual funerals. Immortal in
Their lack of true existence, they stand here
On public show to draw our fear, or trade;

And this way, they shall live for evermore.

1960s

27 The Railings

Once there would have been the woman standing
Between the trees behind the dancing railings as
    he walked,
But that is not now so.

And once there would have been
A hope of the woman, a figment of the branches
As they shifted with the light –
That might have been, that might have been,
But neither is this any longer true.

Not even now is the hope what it was,
And will not regain the face:
Two years, three years, the walk could go
While only the principle of the woman

Faintly remained. And that would scarcely be
    enough.
The principle will drain from out a place.
The hope will have to go to other things.

28 Retirement

The middle-afternoon is the worst of the blanks.
Shuffle the four equal armies of the contentious cards
And manoeuvre those. Or failing that, indict for yourself
In a never-to-be-written recollection, your successful
Colleague of some brisk campaign. The minor consolations
Of the manageable evening arrive the faster
For either, or both, of these applications of power.

29   *Path to the Observatory*

Cramped in parentheses and double negatives,
The hesitant, in others, most respect
Whatever goes most squarely to the point,
And tries to gain much by confronting much.

For the permanent grief of time, they might
      admire
This uncompromising answer, given
By a path going straight across the park
To this famous hub of time:

Hardly nervous, never flinching the effects
Of its bold-faced approach (as dubious lovers
      might).
But challenging time it goes; and chides
The uneven grass nearby, and the ragged trees.

30   *Interlude*

The extended knee, not covered and perhaps
Two feet away across the garden grass
Is as grained and natural as a hand;
Could even be, as a hand is, touched
Without self-consciousness or much design
In a ceremonious gesture, if such existed.
To such size is the thing brought down
By her informal proximity, poised between
That distance and that closeness which both start
Lust. And the urge of talk
Which yesterday broke out in an unwise heat
And tomorrow may impede itself in the throat,
Can be temperate, easily. The sun is out.
An insect travels the pattern of her dress.
The afternoon is calm, with Latin words.

31 *Go Away*

I have come about the ground, is this your ground?
– Go away, I want to kneel by myself
On this first dry patch of the year, and prepare the soil.

That's a right occupation, but my purpose is to warn you
About the ground – Look, a person like me
Has no time to talk. I've only one evening for the garden.

But please, I think your ground may not be safe!
– Yes, but don't come and bother me now. I have bulbs
Which I want to settle in; and there are pebbles to sift out.

Listen, someone is deliberately undermining your garden
– You are worse than the weeds and the greenfly. Go away.
When shall I get these narcissi planted?

But even if you plant them they won't grow. They won't have
Any time to sprout or flower.
– But I've always grown flowers here. Why say things like
        that?

Because the ground is undermined, they are going
To blow it up. – What you're saying is ridiculous.
I trust them, I know they would never do such a thing.

Then who are those men bending down at the edge of the
        garden,
What is this spreading tremor of the ground
That snatches the spade from your hand?

What is wrenching the saplings up? – Why expect me to
        know?
I suppose they must know what they are doing.
I suppose it's for the best. Why don't you go away!

32   *At the Time*

Perhaps the daring made it
Seem all right. Or
The memory of the daring.
At the time, there were
The midges, was the fidgeting
Of bottles in someone's
Crates; all the mere
Ungainliness of limbs:
There was the wanting
To get it done and over,
And to resume a proper,
Acceptable posture.
Only much afterwards, was there
The having done, was there
That person (think of it),
And that place; all the daring
Shame of it. Only afterwards,
That. There was, really,
Nothing at all of this,
Nothing at all, at the time.

33   *1939*

Where the ball ran into the bushes,
And I was sent to find it, being
Useful for that more than to play their game,
I saw instead
This badge, from someone's brother, in
Some regiment of that war: a trophy
Begged for and polished, coveted certainly,
But lost now, slightly touched with dust already,
Yet shining still, under smooth leaves drab with dust.

I knew that people prized such trophies then,
It was the way of all of us. I might,
For no one looked, have taken it
For mine. I valued it. It shone
For me as much as anyone.
And yet some fear or honesty, some sense
It wasn't to be mine – it wasn't more –
Said No to all of this. Besides,
They shouted in the distance for their ball.
For once quite quickly, I
Made up my mind
And left the thing behind.

34 *Farmer's Point of View*

I own certain acre-scraps of woodland, scattered
On undulating ground; enough to lie hidden in. So,

About three times a year, and usually August,
Pairs of people come to one or another patch. They stray

Around the edges first, plainly wanting some excuse
To go on in; then talking, as if not concerned,

And always of something else, not what they intend,
They find their way, by one or another approach,

To conducting sexual liaisons – on *my* land.
I've tried to be careful. I haven't mentioned 'love'

Or any idea of passion or consummation;
And I won't call them 'lovers' because I can't say

If they come from affection, or lust, or blackmail,
Or if what they do has any particular point

For either or both (and who can say what 'love' means?)
So what am I saying? I'd like to see people pondering

What unalterable acts they might be committing
When they step down, full of plans, from their trains or cars.

I am not just recording their tragic, or comic, emotions,
Or even the subtler hazards of owning land –

I am honestly concerned. I want to say, politely,
That I worry when I think what they're about:

I want them to explain themselves before they use my woods.

35 No Good

It is no good if any man dreams
Her love is attainable by schemes:
No one can win these modern wars,
Why squander tactics on this sort of cause?

It is no good if one decides
Love can be bought, extravagance provides:
She will be right to stay unmoved,
Those won those ways may end unloved.

It is no good if, slyly, one defends
Courses her other lover recommends:
Guile with her is out of place,
She can read any hidden face.

It is no good in the rare state
Of abused purity, the discarnate:
She will think stories, and surmise;
Agree, with pity in her eyes.

It is no good pretending your
Passion is an unbreakable law:
She may obey it! You'll be spent
In some obscene predicament.

It is no good any way one takes,
The sin is travel if roads are mistakes,
The plague is feet if it's no good proceeding:
I do not think this is too misleading.

36 *Diana and the Transmitter*

Being below it, well!
There are no words at first.
There is nothing quite like
This bloody great steel tower,

Which won't be a toy,
Or any brick, sensible thing,
But coerces the feeble eye
Up hair-thin ladders

To nominal platforms, thrown
From windy leg to leg
– Where it leaves it, hurt and scared,
To acquire a disturbing thought:

If by any crude, romantic
Ruse of some enemy
I had either to climb that stair
Or never see her again

– To climb to the spiked top,
Or even some lower stage
(And I dread this so much
It's almost probable!) –

I know that I couldn't climb,
Not even for that sake;
And I am so humbled by
Those with heads for heights

Or knowledge of engineering, that
I refuge in defiance,
And uncomfortably strike some right
Attitudes, out of fear; like these:

I rebuke the brisk graduates
Working for this tower
(Reforming, transforming
The medium from inside!)

I reject the proponents of better
Advertising art (those makers
Of terylene haloes for whores)
And the conscience-salvers with Granada.

I will not take the excuses
Of the inexcusables who
Make the animal voices
For cartoons; for whom

This tranquillizing monument
Seems particularly built. And
I question the final moral right
Of this meccano phallus

To landscape, anyway, here.
I'd ask this of Collins,
Orr Stanley, Simms; and would have
Their answers less than smooth.

And look: this is nearly making up
For any earlier lack, out
Of weakness, of any proved love
– If, as I think, these curses

Are gesturing to defend (for want
Of any daring will of mine
To try to climb the thing) her
Every facet of virginity.

37 *Yesterday's Fire*

One lifting tatter of black, burnt paper
Soared up, and stayed, like a raven watching,
On a tree's limb. But I am not deterred
By would-be omens.
                    A hand quite over
A hand, but quietly, is the only start,
And to part her fingers wrong. Properly so
I placed my left hand then.
                            You must be sure
You don't impose some will that gentleness,
Not wanting to offend, might not resist.
I said, I said this carefully,
                              'You may withdraw
Your hand mine holds on if you really wish.'
Just then, a brash wind switching the drifting
Of the smoke our way, we both at once
                                    Jumped back,
Hands kept together; and she did not quite
Disengage till the thing I said
Could be fully taken in. But she understood.
                                        'You must take back
The hand yourself. I do not want to give
You back discourtesies.' And nicely smiled,
'Make it your will – please not my petulance.'
                                            And as I brought

My hand away, I glanced into the tree,
Where, as I looked, I saw that tatter fall,
Which may have made an omen after all.

Strong sleep alone in the house makes all the difference.
It must be a good dull day, though: and no birdsong.
Then sleep enough will set most issues right.

So will the indulgent water of the bath,
Where I lie next, ten reassuring minutes. This
Can render any problem easy, and

I often take a pad in, for jotting solutions,
Putting it with the soap and the torn sponge
On the bath edge; it might be useful.

So it's ten-thirty, and everything is easy
– But now a brash sunlight points out patterns
Of undying dust in air to think about,

Or takes up the steam from the surface of the water
Like rising, drifting smoke. And secondly,
The telephone is arrogantly ringing. There is

Time just for the towel, and to leap downstairs
Past the impending shadow of someone
About to knock at the locked and bolted door.

I have snatched off the receiver of the phone, yet
The thing keeps somehow ringing and ringing.
A fault on the line somewhere? As if I would know!

My sleep was worthless: the caller fidgets and coughs
On the step outside; the phone rings on; the black
Receiver slithers on my sweating ear.

I can formulate two
Excuses in mitigation:
First, blasphemy surely admits
Some firm, good name:

Only the loved names can
Incite to abuse and treasons:
You cannot blaspheme over what
You must despise.

Second it was, of course,
A trick, in assistance of love,
And no truth. This is the plain fact.
To please a spy,

Huge factories are built
With shuddering walls of dark steel
– Shells of deception, all a lie.
My words did that.

Let an amending tongue
Now penitently cast for means
To rebegin flattery, since
I shrink in fear

Of how I have blasphemed
If nothing can be seen to crack
These literal words; unmake
What they imply.

It is with metaphor
We can assuage, abolish and
Create. I will apologize
With metaphors:

Listen: you could not know,
But when the snow dashed your face, it made
Patterns on white, violent glass, stone-
Scattered; and as

Your mouth just opened, now,
In a slight surprise, all the lions'
Mouths on the bronze financial doors
Dropped their gripped rings.

40   *Sunsets*

Suddenly caught by how it seems
Possible and quite credible that,
In this last windless minute at

Sunset, that downspread of fields I watch
(Gazing past, from this vantage hill,
Just visible cows to the town) will

Have darkened a little – even though
You can't measure this, and it may be
Your eyes don't tell it truthfully –

I sense a comparison with
Some points in the progress of love:
Times when each element *has* to move

At just the stage when you would want
It at rest – when, dispassionate
-ly, you would want to define and state

To yourself just where you stand. It may
Be a simple error to believe
That love runs on like that, you can deceive

Yourself quite easily. But
So often love seems to be set
On rushing you past anywhere you get

A chance to arrest it, and talk.
And in this, as with nightfall, you sense
That you cannot make much pretence

Of defying any darkness.
It leaves you no other choice.
It happens in front of your eyes.

41   *By Paul's Kitchen Clock*

He trembles, now, at his spyholes of jealousy. How
Appalling his guessing is! Not even a frost night
And white, hard grass such that their body-spaces would show
As hot, cleared blanks on the indifferent ground where they lay
– This would not have kept them back.
So, knowing what door they must surely re-enter by,
He waits to snatch on any audible step, guessing
Signs on her of hand-marks, in her freed and shaken hair,
And stands ready to be unable to overhear
Words whose meaning he will watch
On their lips, which smile them out; storing for just himself
All of these facts – as politicians learn to cherish
Each act of slander, planning their rivals' overset
With a decayed, set calmness, like the moon's.

Sunlight goes on making
And making its reappearances on that stained wall
Without alteration. It's getting
More elderly, I would say; goes a mellower course
Over chair-dent and sweat-mark,
Moving a window-square which seems
Not so clear now at the edges. To have
Sat once among such motes and specks
Was to be glad to see dust made quick
By illumination, interruption by liveness.
This dust now is literal dust, shown up
By this changed also sun as wandering in air
As thinking wanders in the aged – with
An unkind pleasantness. Such sun
Used not to calm me near to sleep like this.

a junction

Not to meet, then. But can't we maintain
One concessionary contact: of
Some meeting in theory – for instance,
Making an agreement to retain
A *kind* of connection by a glance
Each day at some same landmark? Or have

An intersection of routes planned out
On journeys we are often making?
This could be a place where we again
– At quite different times! – could no doubt
'Meet'; (I would cross it like a night train
Crossing points – rapid, darkened, trembling.)

Sprogo (in the Great Belt)

In that sea-stretch, one minor island,
It makes a misty scrap of jutting
Land from wide water. A calmer green
Covers, though, all but one nearly hand-
Wise gesture of cliff, where can be seen
A caged, rusted lantern, cautioning.

You could be compared with any slim,
Chill, passing thing, at will. Yet, the same,
Let me let this dwindling seamark make
Another image: as, on a whim,
Such a quick distant shape could quite take
The diminuendo of your name.

her drawing

No, this Snow Queen (or Cordelia)
Lies drawn, for you, quite differently;
Is merely some unthinking release
Of a moment's work. Still, I see her
As a projection from your own face,
And think: not knowing, you let her be

Like some taller screen image of your
Own contained precision (thus that high
Glance, your own, muting the hands' gestures).
But as she is yours, I must feel
She is truth itself, all such features
Thrown that large by some flattering eye.

second drawing

A kind of swirl of bracken where curve,
Though static, somewhat ambiguous
Symbols, as if grown part of that ground
Of black-stressed, intricate roots (these leave
The surface at no point, but twist round
And upwards into the dubious

Branches of the plant, form letters, signs
Which could mean your name: such as now bring
My mind quite out, away from this sheet,
Elsewhere in time; past these pencilled lines
To their sudden, living start: your neat
Intent smile, your tensed fingers moving).

concession

Privileged now to see you, tell me
(Because I can't know whether I stare
On some frank, actual thing, that skin
Utterly real, or if I yet see
Only a surface which locks me in
With protective, invisible care

As when one looks out at things through glass)
– Are you like somewhere known with plain sight,
Just as clear as you seem? Or do you
Screen off real knowledge, so letting pass
Everything but the quickest key to
That country of air, your clean daylight?

distance

Invent two rings of falling light; wide
For you in the south and the sun's rage,
But not my light – obliged on a neat
Metal table surface to refer
Only to the black words on this sheet:
Chilled, northern light, bronze-shaded. One page

Written already, lies just outside,
In the fawn dusk of the table-edge,
A failure. Still; I can't stop. Be sure
A thousand mere dark miles won't divide
Fact from longing, break down this posture
Of vain love to a better knowledge.

cliffs

Merely thinking up your name in this
Hazardous high strip and ledge in air
Works a consolation: simply that,
Repeating you, any daring is
Practically possible – leant flat
On this shuddering wall, I can stare

Down on the mapped rocks, or out to sea
Unfrightened. Yet in some safe room to
Hear those syllables. . . . The difference
Scares and drowns out all talking for me.
There is no quick courage helps with this
Unexpected way of meeting you.

epistemology

My same eyes once jumped through the page-long
Paragraphs, flickering over such
Banks of abstract words! A *physical*
Power those words had, that caught the strong
Breath of the mind away. The real
Equivalent, now, is your face. Much

That same way your eyes glance this as mine
Glanced; which now face to your forehead's small
Shades and meanings, seek to sublime this
Craving in verbal charts, and refine
Its enigma in a healing verse:
Neurotic; and metaphysical.

44 *The Preservation*

It's quite worth keeping your surprise at the untrodden
Snow on the long step that particular winter night
– As if we had been indoors for days –

As in that time your every movement told,
And looked responsible. Never had your feet
Set out their marks on things with such grave care,

Or honour of any place. And all the mocking
Extensions to words in your hands' actions
Drained right away, or were absolved

In one cupped, simple gesture, collecting
(To taste and to smile) some snow in a quick mild heap
From the near top of the street wall.

45 *Incident in Milan*

They are going about it now
In such silence; yes,
In the garden even:
Bringing to its end
By mutual disagreement
Their long, long liaison
– The line-clothed girl
And the Italian, Maurielli.

45

Such a long drag of
Time were they united,
By their only difference:
Of sex; in all else
Being the same, two
Mere stones of dullness,
Solidly grating
Surfaces in talk, talk.

She would elbow
Past him in the kitchen,
And resent the obtruding
Angle of his chair;
She might push his hair
Accidentally out of
The neatness he once
Contrived for her

And then, from habit, kept (he
Hating her, truly,
For that, and glaring
Back to her trim food
– Insulting in the
Gourmet's care with which
She set it out, between . . .)
The violences of

These inarticulates,
Their moments of hounding truth,
Have no Method dignity,
Really. Are more like
Abandoned sandflats where
No one lives, or ploughs.
Close your own shutters. Read
Or sleep. Let them alone.

46   God's Creatures

We all hate the sturdy nobility
Of the horse, we mock at it in cartoons
And carnivals. Such set, single-minded
Devotion we parody most with the
Two halves of the pantomime animal,
At odds which way to lurch.
                              Somewhere I once
Saw a pseudo-horse climb up to the high
Diving board at a big swimming gala,
Hesitate on the edge, unfunnily,
Then slough off to become two boring frogs
Which grossly flopped through the chlorinated
Air into the water while we watched,
And indulged in human play at the deep end.

47   Warm People

Where complete light is so
narrow it lasts – for six
weeks – all the twenty-four
hours, it's obvious that
window ledges should fill
with tentacle creepers,
or freak geraniums
should front the Arctic with
some days' brash petals. . . .

                                                    But
            I would need it explained
            why, where eight months of
            the fecund calendar
            flowers crowd the out-of-doors,
            people still nurse blooms for
            their cramped houses, lodge them
            in pots and boxes round
            every piled room (while
            leaves cram the windows up
            outside.) Is there a point
            in their insistence on
            this claustrophobia
            of growth?
                        It wouldn't be
            their claim to one success?

48   *A Hairdresser's*

        Something I remember from six is
        Waiting for mother to dry, sat with
        Home Chat and knitting books to read while
        The warm cage glowed round her settled hair.

        That was in a corner up in a
        Room above the Gentlemen's Saloon,
        Out of the way. But they *exhibit*
        Them now, as here, turning magazines

        Under the gesturing fingers of
        Their talkative priestesses. Tall glass
        In the High Street, florid with pot-plants,
        Sets the new style: Huge, groomed photographs

48

And offers of 'Life restored'. It's a
'Fine art', you couldn't relate it to
Any usefulness; in this, having
Less of a function, even, than some

Oildom's backscratcher, following his
Chevrolet to the gaming tables
In a Super Snipe. I wish to feel
My complaint is better than a mere

Chafing memory of a child's hours
Waiting and waiting; it sees the point
With a cool rationality; it has
The courage to reject some things. . . .

But – 'If they want to', drones out some
Fool-libertarian voice, 'let them. Why
Shouldn't they do as they like?' (You
Have heard – or maybe used – that very tone!)

Passing in High Street rain, I repeat
My glance at that window and its line
Of faces locked in hives. No. I can't
Wish I were as liberal as that.

49 *Common Sense*

An agricultural labourer, who has
A wife and four children, receives 20s a week.
¾ buys food, and the members of the family
Have three meals a day.
How much is that per person per meal?
                    – *From Pitman's Common Sense Arithmetic, 1917*

A gardener, paid 24s a week, is
Fined 1/3 if he comes to work late.
At the end of 26 weeks, he receives
£30.5.3. How
Often was he late?

— From Pitman's Common Sense Arithmetic, 1917

A milk dealer buys milk at 3d a quart. He
Dilutes it with 3% water and sells
124 gallons of the mixture at
4d per quart. How much of his profit is made by
Adulterating the milk?

— From Pitman's Common Sense Arithmetic, 1917

The table printed below gives the number
Of paupers in the United Kingdom, and
The total cost of poor relief.
Find the average number
Of paupers per ten thousand people.

— From Pitman's Common Sense Arithmetic, 1917

An army had to march to the relief of
A besieged town, 500 miles away, which
Had telegraphed that it could hold out for 18 days.
The army made forced marches at the rate of 18
Miles a day. Would it be there in time?

— From Pitman's Common Sense Arithmetic, 1917

Out of an army of 28,000 men,
15% were
Killed, 25% were
Wounded. Calculate
How many men there were left to fight.

— From Pitman's Common Sense Arithmetic, 1917

These sums are offered to
That host of young people in our Elementary Schools, who
Are so ardently desirous of setting
Foot upon the first rung of the
Educational ladder . . .

— From Pitman's Common Sense Arithmetic, 1917

Wednesdays were guest night in the mess, when the colonel
expected the married officers, who usually dined at home, to attend.
The band played Gilbert and Sullivan music behind a curtain. . . .
Afterwards the bandmaster was invited to the senior officers' table
for his complimentary glass of Light or Vintage.

(Good-bye to All That)

At the officers' table, for half an hour afterwards, port,
The bandmaster. He accepts, one drink long,
All the courtesy of the gentlemen. They are suave, and equal.
'I expect with your job . . . Do you find . . . Oh well. . .'
The bandmaster edges the shining inch of port along the grain
     of the table,
Precisely covering one knot with the transparent
Base of the glass. He crouches forward over the polished wood
Towards the officers, not comfortably convivial,
Eyes always going to the face speaking next,
Deferential, very pleased.
The band put away their instruments out at the back, having
Drunk their beers, standing.
The detachable pieces of brass lie down
In the felt grooves of the cases, just as they should.
Nine-thirty strikes.
There is laughter of men together, coming from inside.
'Mitchell's still in there, hob-nobbing with the officers.'

51   *A Sunday Breakdown*

Crossing the coarse pebbles with scrupulous tread, in
His Gracechurch Street clothes, poor Ludbrook
Goes out on that long jutting wall to the end point
– Where, evilly foamless and smooth, the sea
Lurches over it – and sits down with his *Times*
Where it's three inches deep, and puts his umbrella up

And waits (reading the Court Circular and Birthdays Today)
For the police, or the lifeboatmen, or the Civil Defence
To be the first to come and argue that what
He does is irrational or dangerous,
And would he stop because he ceases to amuse,
And he is driving away the custom from the place.

52 Trio

He has now gone with the toy gun into the greengrocer's shop
And is using some mock ploy with the greengrocer's girl.
She is cramped up, uncomfortably half-sat on the long ledge
Of the frozen food Cool Cabinet. She looks
A suitable imitation of absolute fright, she raises
Her hands and gives a visible but inaudible shout
– The traffic is so loud – as he gestures with the Xmas gun
Towards the celery or the till. She is a tall excitable
Girl of the kind wearing tinted, attenuated glasses
And patchy coloured nails. He is a thick, blunt, overcoated
Wedge of a middle-class man with several parcels,
Including the toy gun. Now suddenly the proprietor, in a green
    coat,
Comes out of the store at the back and throws a horrified stare,
And shrinks himself, trembling, against the potatoes
In their brown, stolid banks. The man with the wooden red gun
Speaks, you can see, but you can't hear anything he says,
And all of them are standing in these postures still,
As they might be if the gorgon glance of a photographer
Had taken them all in flagrant tableau to present to the future:
On Xmas Eve, behind the green leaves and pink paper
Of the lighted trade window of 'Mackin's Best Fruit', between
Frozen plaice fillets and South African oranges.

53   The Lost Surprise

Your dog I hate strains from you and would run.
A dead-leaf dust confirms the arid grass.
My eyes, faint from newsprint, watch some odd man
Prowl round and round in a feigned casualness
– Voyeur, today, of different lovers. How
Could we two serve such curious interests now?

And yet I think you brought the dog in case:
He was your good excuse lest I should move.
Not that he would protect, but just increase,
By simply sitting there, your chance to have
Some breaking sentence said: he could run loose
At any tiresome moment you might choose.

I have to relish, though, this flattery
You build for both of us; that dares to claim
That lost surprise you need for you to be
My main quest still, the reason that I came;
And brings this dog out on our autumn day
Squatting its aged cunning in the way.

54   The Suggestion

Consideration says you lose a moth by sliding a card
Under a quick glass shut on the wall patch where it sits
And carrying it out, perhaps to a light, to the midnight street.

I am saying to you, then, have understanding ready to devise
Your equivalent trick: get friends, have activities ready to
     divert me
Coming, unignorable and restless, to fret your neat room.

55   *The Victory*

I think it's yours. Furrowing the
Sweat-nights groping for metaphors
– Like the bed's cool patches –
It was hope even then. And other fluences

Carried me somewhere: as, telepathy:
Winging blind wires to carry somehow
News to you. Mad, but it all allowed
The thing to continue. Now, though,

The wires are down. My brain can't ever seem
To stop still enough to think you. My
Bland words talk alone about themselves.
It's yours, this victory, then,

By simple waiting. And, if only you
Might find just what you truly wish through
That same patience – building where
You use it now to reap such disrepair.

56   *The Situation*

For it was that the cousins never came,
And so we could not know what they were like.
They never did walk out in their overwhelming way
To stand by the streaming water-butt, or
To hold the fence with their girls' adult hands.
This garden can't be remembered having them laughing,
So they remain a possibility:
That after our disappointment with man
And with dogs and with travel and with remaining still,
From our last armchairs we shall come to know
That there are the cousins left; who, that day,
Were to come, and did not, and are there to be tried yet.

57   In Crystal Palace Park

One January day, among full frail light:
The new stadium shut in blessed silence; sun,
Of the mild midwinter, glossing the gorilla's haunches;
The lake-sheet above the refreshment-room staying
Quiet, through the trees, as the Consort's white elk facing it.

But slumped and crooked at coffee, I think: Only
Beings like these trees can renew. Teachers or foresters
Could point out endless ring on new ring of survival;
Rafters are told of, whining in sympathy with storms;
Gateposts have launched unearthly leaves; and our Commission's

Dense, patterned groves elsewhere grow for when we are all dead.
Trees outlast us. Seasons – how many have *we?* – make no
        difference
To them, through centuries of vegetable time. – Yet use
Your human reason. Should we feel outfaced by even
These mere park glades, in all their bareness now?

At these moments of disquiet, take any single
Individual tree: your face (you can feel the grooved bark on)
Can almost defy it: for after ten years you can
Think its wear equalling yours. Even the inexpert eye
Can spot decay (like your own: each sad spring bravery of leaves

Seems like the brashness of rejuvenation drugs.)
And then you, councillors, murderers, can ride over
A Preservation Order; or citizen, set your crudest pedigree dogs
To do their natural work at some one tree. It surely was
As abstract 'trees' they had that lasting look.

– It's late. I leave the coffee cup, and step out warily
To the mild air again. Away from gulls, many separately
Walking the grass as one to some unattained place,
I hunch, and stride downhill. And pass each tree,
Not blessed with human reason, living its sober term.

55

Then why see it? This 'flat and ample
Space over which you walk at no one angle,
Led as by something very like your will?'

*You could go on with proper concerns. You
Are boiling tea, typing some letter, listening
To politics when it comes. Why let it, why let*

It come? – That pale, clean stretch
Stays small, and won't usurp the whole. So
I let it come. There is no harmful freedom.

*But where do you go across that space? Do you
See things, see anyone?* I don't go anywhere
But across it; taut and clear, though the wind leans at me.

Further, it might be a world, and not safe:
It might be stayed in. I keep it unfulfilled.
Its colour? Certain shadows, shades of green.

– And whoever she who walks there, and stands,
She won't tremble into definition, isn't
Like Fournier's girl, say, on the steps and real.

Then why let it come at all? Only, that to this
All common facts yearn to approximate,
While time strains to reach it. And it

Won't be otherwise, it refuses, and must
Return as plainly as before; nothing but
A kind of sober walking-space. – I see

You are not answered why, nor sense why I let it come.

Pain of the leaf, one two –
Word of the stone, three, four –
Foot of the dark, pit of the hand,
Heart of the cloud, five, six, and
Out!
  Skip.
Nora she had white eyes,
Mary she had black –
Helen looked in Grey Man's Wood and
Never came
Back!
  Jump.
Nora draws a green thread,
Mary spins it blue –
But Helen will not bind it till her
True Love makes it
True!
  Quick!
One, two, leaf of the pain,
Three, four, stone of the word,
Five, six, dark of the foot, hand of the pit,
Cloud of the heart, and
OUT!

60 *Nasty Habit*

The sky is so white, the paper is so white.
The unattended leaves of January lie in the damp.
The girl who ran upstairs wrote
Her face, pausing, on the blank of the white wall
(Or on my eyes) with black and pointed hair.
That clock is very fast, the time exists.

And, well, the emotional components exist
For something; for one of the three or four
Attempts at answering 'loneliness'.
Here is a chair comfortable for meditation,
Arms long enough to stretch on, back facing
Towards the window and concealing any

Thought or action I might have or take.
It's up to me. I can sense the moral framework
Even now expanding to allow
A lot of things. Virtually every gesture
Takes on its altruistic look, and
'I had to do it . . .' feels an honourably

Far-off last resort. . . . So I start to write.

61 *Office Party*

We were throwing out small-talk
On the smoke-weary air,
When the girl with the squeaker
Came passing each chair.

She was wearing a white dress,
Her paper-hat was a blue
Crown with a red tassel,
And to every man who

Glanced up at her, she leant over
And blew down the hole,
So the squeaker inflated
And began to unroll.

She stopped them all talking
With this trickery,
And she didn't leave out anyone
Until she came to me.

I looked up and she met me
With a half-teasing eye
And she took a mild breath and
Went carefully by,

And with cold concentration
To the next man she went,
And squawked out the instrument
To its fullest extent.

And whether she passed me
Thinking that it would show
Too much favour to mock me
I never did know –

Or whether her withholding
Was her cruelty,
And it was that she despised me,
I couldn't quite see –

So it could have been discretion,
And it could have been disgust,
But it was quite unequivocal,
And suffer it I must:

All I know was: she passed me,
Which I did not expect
– And I'd never so craved for
Some crude disrespect.

You said you couldn't
Do other. You were
That conventional
You just walked 'into
The night.' It hurled rain.

They had left on the
Light in the builders'
Yard to stop burglars,
And you had eight wet
Miles' ride. But what was

Not usual was (and
I didn't know) you
Carried a man's child
Two months uninter-
rupted away in

You. It wasn't mine,
I loved you, and by
This bit of chance, your
Not telling me, you
Left, to take her on

Till birth, and to push
Her onwards down time
To stand here (a child
Two months in her too,
Which I do know, and

The new child not mine
Either) where the light
Left on in that yard
Again shows me that
Shape I love, as we

Look at your photo
She holds (bit of chance!)
And I wonder if,
After all these dark
Things, I'll let *her* leave.

63   *Affinity*

He. This thing we have, one means by it what starts
    Between two people not near to one another
    Who have hardly met and never spoken,
    Yet know some faint intangible linking
    – Neither to be made firm, nor yet to be broken.

She. I don't see it like this at all, but
    In opposites: a sudden image of this woman,
    Myself, set off on this dark road unaccompanied,
    Pacing between blank hedges, her feet
    Leaving and reaching echoes, behind and ahead,

    And all at once this new thing arriving,
    The darkness thinning and varying, the car
    Rushing the channels of her ear, its light
    Climbing the sides of trees. And her one doubt is to
    Ask what *kind* of man he is at the wheel that night

    (Is he lover, enemy, casual messenger,
    To give all her landscape that white leaping look?)
    Since although she cowers back in the mist, bent
    In self-protecting fear of what he means,
    She has called and craved for . . . this new element.

64   *Ode to Felix*

At that tired eye-level point where
Impulse buying starts, he
Was there in flush, banked rows in
The supermarket: Felix the Cat.

Two dozen cat-food packets, patterned
For sales appeal, repeated two
Dozen static gestures of his face who
Almost first made cartoons animate.

I remembered that black-and-white
Stroll, brought back on the t.v. screen
About twenty years after: undoubtedly
Smart for its time, the commentator said.

Yes, he had all the possibilities
Already, little early Felix. His
Famous walk was even then the quaint, quick
Cartoon swagger, his features were

The easy prototype of all
Those smirking descendants, capering
In slick, flourished lines, richer
For the primary colours, and running on

Down and down a million celluloid frames
Hand-painted in endless studio rows by
Patient, paid artists reducing everything to
That clear-cut, lucid world, while

Elsewhere other grown men sound-tracked
The basic squawk. – This way was
The world infested by your
Charming animal kingdom, Felix, having

Driven out real beasts. Numberless
American children responded to
The uncle-funny voices, actually came
To look like Mickey Mouse. In the

Demure eyes of innumerable
Homely girls and wives lived
Bambi's primal innocence. Felix,
You were first of all those lovably

Blundering and resourceless dogs and
Elephants who helped to make our
Gross and failing natures bearable.
You set off Li'l Abner, firm and strait,

Shouldering over fields with no effort, as in
Our own fulfilment dreams, you
Tamed with Snow White all our dwarfs
And witches, you helped to paint

Donald Duck on the fuselage of
The bomber for Hiroshima. If today
A man in the *Sunday Times* Colour
Supplement makes t.v. commercials

To pay to make his very own cartoon
Satirizing agencies, the credit's
Partly yours, and you can be proud to think your
Walt Disney voted for Goldwater . . .

I would not buy your food, I have no cat.
I can pass on down the stacked and shining
Aisles to other violences (the frozen red
Chops glossed in cellophane on puce, plastic trays)

But I'm not to pass without that sense, again,
Of one of my more elementary sorts of
Going mad: Your thousands of representatives,
Felix, walking into my world, writing my

Morning letters, modulating from the shapes
Of strangers outside the house, answering
My alarm calls for Fire, Police, *Ambulance*. In
That last nightmare trap and maze, they

Strut and chirp their obscene, unstoppable
Platitudes, Felix, while I run round and
Round and round to destroy their pert, joking smiles
And scream my own voice hoarse into their cute squeak.

65   *Incident on 6th August*

Last and most hurting stroke of the wide,
Inescapable sunlight, a flash from some turning car's windscreen
Streaks across to my eyes and blots the whole day black.

I walk on looking out through a pulsing cloud
At the disfigured street, planting a
Seething blur on every face and dress:

They move, half-black and writhing, towards me,
Not knowing, in their late afternoon. They
Are talking and smiling and conducting their

Own concerns beneath my surface of wounds. And
Who am I to tell them they are
Scorched blotches in an insane ignorance?

They would think me the mad one.

She lifts up her fawn head, nodding
Rapidly into air; she rests tensing, then
Untensing fingers on the table-top;
She closes her eyes;
And she counts, counts, with a flicker of lips breathing,
In a sort-of ecstasy of computation
– Which she gets wrong.

Such processes of icy reckoning
Seem somehow endangered by this
Devotion of her complete creatureness; by which
She renders her whole, quick, committed
Pulse to contradict all
Numeration's neat sterility:
The figures tremble as they add and rise.

And it seems all the more wrong that
We worry to put in the programming that
Conscious suffusion of some
Warmth like this, alleged to make
All the clean lights and unagitated
Dials tolerable.
While it looked only wise to bring

This human mildness in somewhere,
We should have known the struggle
Long lost before anyone ever
Began on those cool, implacable
Constructs of order and tabulation
– Clicking us into place like straight
White sticks crossed on mass graves –

And should have sensed that to
Start so late, even, was as to
Wake up that fallible, routine sentinel
To see the gulls' possible
Missile flight over his waiting screen, and
In his cavern room, to lift
His one telephone, once.

67   *Winter Appointment*

Now, after too long,
A fool's courage flows back again, and assists me
To the dentist's chair and his unheavenly lights.

The vanished space between me and this house has been
Like the gap scaring
Some anxious lover and all that he dared not risk.

Horse, hawk and debutante in the smooth magazines
Soothe, in the waiting-room, me, with tired coat and grey
Mouth. Rising, I think:

Scales of sharp justice
Appear to be carefully balancing this out:
For those gropings at pleasure, this payment of pain.

Two weeks gone since my first daring venture, when I
Knew he would not start,
And I only need fearfully submit to that

Quick, sinister, flicking parade of the wan street
Of my mouth, that tilting of searching mirrors, prods
At each drab structure,

Surveyor's verdict:
No site to be cleared, or buildings to be shored up,
Though some cleaning, for appearances, would improve.

But! – *I'll take a small X-ray of that one, in case . . .*
And two weeks of fright
Till today's visit, even if swift certainty

Soon now. (Yes . . . take a large X-ray of Diana,
I'd still not know what meant reassurance and
What shaking terror.)

★

So. Today's the day . . .
Well, I *could* have shirked it . . . What more helpful than to
Put off yet another painful self-attrition?

Do sit. Bleak time of revealing: no comfort here.
A train grates, roars down
The cutting outside, the smooth cat flops off the sill.

Something will have to be done . . . You see there was this
Shadow like a sin I didn't think I might have
On the X-ray plate.

Nothing but to *sit*
As the cotton wool dabs at the affronted gums
And his white arm slopes to the swivel tray. But – please –

Talk, please – Rhodesia, anything – till the
Injection takes . . . I'll
Lie open-mouthed at the honour of van der Byl.

A sort-of napkin fitted below my neck. 'Not
Where he eats, but where . . .' (Diana-pray-grace-this-meal-
Before-and-during!)

. . . Christ! anything *must*
Be painful to be salutary. His foot pumps
The chair close (think of her, think of her, think of her,

67

Seize her presence with some poet's metaphysical
Calling of her to
This moment: for example, though he be a man

I'll allow Diana to visit the dentist:
His drill is the one of all the violations
Which purges and mends.)

Jarring suddenness;
Intermission; recommencement. *Take a good rinse.*
We are come now, I would say, to the nub of this . . .

Pain accurately descends his cold, angled crane
Of quivering wires:
Bleak hysteria of the burr changing its note.

*

And how long do these renewals last? What hope place
In his painful skill, or in any curative
Promise I might have?

There are no answers;
Except to make a quick leap in equivocal
Relief and faith from his chair, and, to myself, say

That to have no trust in tooth mended or promise
Kept, helps no raw nerve . . .
A cavity clear, metal could firm in the space.

A sure, pure flame melted his amalgam. At last
He has carved a surface, he has stripped that napkin
Away; so I rise,

Convinced. With ball-point
I fray his dotted line, sense comfort in the gift
Of this restored street in hopeful mid-afternoon,

Down which Diana could be ready softly to
Walk, as down some now-
Cleansed and part-shuttered Piccadilly, quite alone.

68   *Hedonist*

It was not the religious pleasure-principle,
The supposed, long quest of the libertine; nor
Was it any kind of arrant desire for
Immolation in some seizing mode of brief
Forgetfulness. It was no sort of strained belief,
Or meditated act; but much more simple:

It was the sense of the sufficient good-ness
Of the next thing beyond the present thing:
The food after a day not eating,
The landing after the stairs, the prospect of some
Prospect filling the ten next minutes, should they come.
It was sleep, sometimes. But simpler even than these,

It could be just the sunlight, as an amiable event
To walk out into after the thick
Complexities of his room, leaving cigarettes, stick
And tablets and trusting, for once,
To his own feet and the friendliness of distance,
And to mere walking alone on the bright pavement.

69   *Old Company*

What is there underneath this tight and
Scarlet creasing at their eye-corners,
As the mouth-stretching laughter-spasm holds
And stacks each man's entire, shuddering
Body on top of his stomach folds?

Their faces seize in this concerted anguish.
The spread-out, cumbersome limbs around the circle
Look like helpless pain to possess.
But they will laugh, and stay. Their risen steam
Muffles each window, hides the street's greyness.

Gregarious mankind . . . Old company
Can ride down any fear as the stale
Seconds of their present unendurably tear
Them piecemeal away from those fresher
Seconds of their mutual past, where

The first laugh started. Each one's ageing face
Makes now a shield for his flesh, here where
All shields grip together grimacing
On phalanx-night against the terror
In one expressionless, unchanging thing.

70 *Song*

The pheasants rightangle away into the thicket;
The mill sails appear on the right, as the map ventures;
The sedge bends to the light wind politely, not constrained;
                    I love you as detail.

The church has a tower the miniature of its tower;
Finished sacks, thrown down, glitter and litter on the field;
Three day-owls scatter towards the approaching wood;
                    I love you for detail.

The lane turns into two ruts with a thick grass centre;
Rides of pines come thinly down to entreat at the hedge;
Hay-blocks provide for the month under polythene sheets;
                    I love you in detail.

Turned soil rests and waits in the damp, clean and unharried;
The concealing flat cloud glows, in foreground to the sun;
One gust flicks beads of wet from the grass at crazed angles;
                    I love you through detail.

71 *Disposed to Sleep*

To cry, in the near space
Between the unfolded pale screen and the bed,
Would be late, late; and would be water only.
My fluids have been less, always,
Than that impartial, other blood which now
Drips from poised foresight into
The channels under his skin.
I have not given, this or other ways.
I have, like this, gone in and out
Of bad sleep, not grasping;
Working
Dry-lip-words to half-recognize
Those faces, what they came for.
                              And here the dark sister
Stands too soon by my own breathing side.

72 *Fourth Lover*

That fourth lover you mentioned, the dangerous one
Only to be talked about carefully, the one
Closest of all, still: him I will not demote too far.

I may even be generous, and allow him
One small particular duchy in
The Holy Empire of your consciousness.

Its name? – Insomniac nostalgia.

73   *Mad Animals*

In comic, unthreatening circles, the spaniel
Ran mad and fretted round the college cat;
Which sat still and just, only, looked

With at most a mild, unequivocal
Compassion. What this spaniel did was a
Sort of obsessed, yelping, bewildered

Orbit of this inexplicable creature
For a long time. It was not dignified. It was
An insanity, reproached and warned by

The gargoyles on the chapel gutter, who
Presented like frenzies, punished with
Being congealed in stone and permanent.

This was a cat of super-elegance; and
O spaniel, you to have no dignity,
Dog as you are, and self-possessed really!

What use was it to yelp? – And yet, and yet,
On an inside page in Rees-Mogg's *Times* there was,
Against all reason, news and a picture of

A cat some man had bred with spaniel's ears.

74   *Pathetic Fallacy*

Now autumn's rank enforcement of
Fawn-pointed thistle and tip-faded iris
Leaves us with this garden as an
Indifferent waste, we tend to let it alone;
We tend to light the rooms early.

We dispose to think mostly indoors, for
Outdoors only stay the limited
Tactics of inanimate things: the stray
Of blown leaves from the heap, dabs of rain
Blurring the fences, grass become irrelevant.

Nothing to think about there, we think.
Let's hug to itself the self of winter,
Glad of the close fire's flattery, happy
For winds to slam doors on us as if
It was worlds happening against our very will.

75 *Balls of Sweetness*

Before James Carra knew Anne Furlington
She made love, often, the first in both their lives,
Under a slipping mauve quilt in a seaport,
With nightlong traffic noise disturbing;
There being wallpaper the same as in her
College room; and it was Peter Daines.
It was the world. No one seemed later hurt, or
Finally betrayed.
                    It was not of consequence.

When Hester Lang told Cavan Benther that
Hidden in some long spell away from him was
A week when Philip Quernier was prepared
And it happened three times (but each time one of them
Pretended) an hour was enough for Cavan's
Fury. Nor were these people heartless. It was
Not of consequence. Such oddness at such distance
Could be healed.
                    It was the world.

73

Elizabeth Pender felt that past could be
Contentedly left as past concerning
William Stennett's beds where Margaret Bourn
Fought conscience and hindering fear. She
Only nodded; and thought. Such guileless frankness
Gave a lot of help. This would leave
No injury-traces . . . It was the world. In minutes
Their hands came coolly together.
                              It was not of consequence.

76   *For my Son*

Not ever to talk when merely requested,
Not ever to be the performing child,
This is what you would establish;
                        always keeping
Private and awkward counsel against
All coaxing; and going – one hopes –
The way of a good will,

To your own true designs. Which is
The way of some human institutions,
Growing not as any collective urge
                        would have them
(In its own placable image) but into
Their own more wayward value – strong,
Untidy, original, self-possessed.

77 Twenty-Third Day

The moon, a rejected
Gift to your disconsolate nature,
Is wasting on you its good literary

Pause in the elm branches across the river;
So that your hand leaves mine on principle, and
Complains that I make you too much the moon,
An uncomfortable ideal . . .

There is, in that, a kind of unguessed truth.
One knows, by now, the moon to be
Pock-marked, with routine mountains; thick
With feet-deep uninteresting dust
Which chokes its incursors; and worse,
She is attainable for the worst of motives.

In all, she is only a little, pale thing,
Ordinary, and human in her way (going through
Phases? You have your bloody ones; sometimes.)

– And only just staying, through inflictions
Of time and knowledge, the same, white,
Round-faced, acceptable creature.

78 *In the Room Above*

In their bed of loss they are
Like sea-things.

Her cries, like drifting gulls',
Lie ancient and somehow
Small about the air, as if wanting
Unction or pity.

A metropolis sways outside,
But in their surge of two griefs they are
Not disturbed.

– I think I know why pity comes to mind.

There was her choosing to cry,
Which she had heard was so; and there was you.

It was your silence, silence,
Made her lost and bird voice pitiful.

79   *Pictures*

Terror at night, that turns precise:
Sweat of the firebell chills my skin
With fear you lie in swathes of smoke
Too dense for rescuers to break in.

I could fling back the sheets at two,
Shake myself into waking and
Run all the roads half-clothed to where
That gaping ignorance would stand

Watching your slimness, blanket-wrapped,
Handled down ladders into the snow
As I recall those bodies were,
Was it four Boxing Nights ago?

– But then, mortality extends
To any step in any street:
There's dog-bite, or there's poison in
What small amounts of food you eat.

'Friendship is lovely' – yes, but who
Knows of all opening doors which one
Closes in velvet kindliness
And stands you facing someone's gun?

This way, the horrors flock around,
The fears come pestering. – And yet
Their idiot multiplicity
Provides a kind of safety-net:

If I decide sometimes to dread
Your falling down on every stair,
Just as irrationally I could
Think you strode safely anywhere.

If death could wait on any step,
Conversely you might stay intact
From any earthly wound or stain
Your sort-of innocence might attract.

And leaving every profitless
Anxiety which coats the breath:
There is one fantasy I feel
A *little* likelier than death:

A day in sultry weather, soon,
To sit and think, idly, to where
Some momentary fatigue has bent
Your shoulders . . . With a casual air

You stretch; and all that row of beads
Rides upwards on your stretching dress
– My fingers stretch out miles to touch
Their spacing red-and-yellowness.

Would this aspiring gesture set
Some small telepathy in train?
Encouraged by the thought, I go
And try the telephone, again.

– Anna's voice. You are called. Downstairs
You answer with far-off surprise,
Slow, as you yawn and curse, to see
Anything with your naked eyes.

You take your glasses from the shelf,
Hold, and unfold, them, to the light,
Flick them across your sleeve, and put
Them on, so that your world seems right,

– And speak. Although you often hate
Suggestions made when you are tired,
This time some sixth and lucky sense
Tells you what answer is required.

Distance can cancel out itself,
But slowly! Thought is faster than
Speeds at which engines or mere feet
Can move to carry any man.

But finally your street, too warm
Under that gathering summer cloud,
Arrives. And when the intercom
Takes up your syllable aloud,

The lock releases. As my steps
Run to the inner door upstairs,
You stack some records on, and make
To rearrange the couch and chairs . . .

Some time earlier in the week,
We cleaned this room. These cushions take
A gentler attitude, one feels,
For every kind and prescient shake.

The window's wide. You jump to see
Your curtains snatched into the storm,
But something lucky I think to say
Makes laughter of your half-alarm.

The Indian shade veiling the lamp
Clicks, in the draught which shuts the door.
Anna is out. The phone is dead.
You nudge four shoes towards the floor.

Braceleted and bare, your arm
Stretches to drop on a low shelf
Your folded glasses. How the rain slants.
Gently the record plays itself.

That table-lamp again. It has
Horsemen mounting a fawn hill.
The edge of its hushed arc of light
Quivers; and yet the draught is still.

There are some fish that drift about
And at each breathing close their eyes,
As if replenishments of air
Came each on each a sweet surprise . . .

No matter . . . Half-an-hour in one track
– A kind of blues, but sweet enough –
The automatic pick-up arm
Achieves its end and switches off.

Much social detail you don't need.
Fuller descriptions of the flat?
Or names, or times, or what we drank?
Invent your own. And leave it that

As well as pictures in each eye
We get slipped discs and are let lie
In some large, liberal, hospital
Bed together, so that all

The learned doctors might come near
(Oh, not to diagnose, but) to hear
Wild, whimsical, allusive range
Of talk, on questions rich and strange

For, laid on boards to straighten us
For all things curved and tortuous,
Day upon day we languish there
And talk, from Twardzik to Voltaire.

80   *Breaking Eggs*

It is as if she chose to exist
To scathe forgivable sins
– In which she could be right;

But to watch her way, for example,
With pardonable pride, or any faintly
False dignity or ceremoniousness

Is somehow terrible.
                         And to prepare a meal
(Though no one should dare to asperse her skill),
She will unclasp each poised, mature

Vegetable's grip upon itself, leaf
By pathetic leaf, intently; or crack
The fragile and decorous eggs

With rapid and curt fingers, not smiling.
It would look like no more than cold spite
If it were not her own kind of care; and

If she could not also, with a mere knife only,
Take up (precise and chilling miracle!)
Each omelette into surging fabric-folds.

Turn on the tap for straight and silver water in the sink,
Cross your finger through
The sleek thread falling
                    – *One.*

Spread white sandgrains on a tray,
And make clean furrows with a bent stick
To stare for a meaning
                    – *Two.*

Draw some clumsy birds on yellow paper,
Confronting each other and as if to fly
Over your scribbled hill
                    – *Three.*

Cut rapid holes into folded paper, look
At the unfolded pattern, look
Through the unfolded pattern
                    – *Four.*

Walk on any square stone of the pavement,
Or on any crack between, as long
As it's with no one or with someone
                    – *Five.*

Throw up a ball to touch the truest brick
Of the red–brick wall,
Catch it with neat, cupped hand
                    – *Six.*

Make up in your head a path, and name it,
Name where it will lead you,
Walk towards where it will lead you
                    – *Seven.*

One, two, three, four, five, six, seven:
Take-up-the-rag-doll-quietly-and-sing-her-to-sleep.

This coarse road, my road, struggles out
South-east across London, an exhausted
Grey zigzag of stubborn, unassimilable
    Macadam, passing hoardings pasted

With blow-ups of cricket journalists, blackened
And not-quite-Georgian terraces,
Shagged-out Greens of geraniums and
    Floral coats-of-arms, lost pieces

Of genteel façade behind and above
Lyons' shopfronts and 'Pullum Promotions',
– Journeying between wired-off bombed lots glossy
    With parked Consuls, making diversions

Round bus depots and draggled estates
In circumlocutory One-Ways,
Netting aquaria in crammed pet store windows,
    Skirting multi-racial bingo queues,

And acquiring, for its self-hating hoard, old black-railed
Underground bogs advising the Seamen's Hospital,
'Do-it-yourself' shops, 'Funerals and Monuments', and
    Victorian Charrington pubs. All

Along its length it despoils, in turn, a sequence
Of echoless names: Camberwell, Peckham,
New Cross Gate; places having no recorded past
    Except in histories of the tram.

It takes out, in cars, arterial affluence
At week-ends, returning it as bad blood
To Monday mornings in town. It is altogether
    Like a vein travelled by hardy diseases, an aged

Canal dredgeable for bodies left behind
On its soulless travels: Sixty-Nine,
Thirty-Six, One-Eight-Five. It takes no clear
    Attitude anyone could easily define

So as to resist or admire it. It seems to hate you
Possessively, want to envelop you in nothing
Distinguishable or distinguished, like its own
    Smothered slopes and rotting

Valleys. This road, generally, is one for
The long-defeated; and turns any ironic
Observer's tracer-isotope of ecology,
    Sociology, or hopeful manic

Verse into a kind of mere
Nosing virus itself. It leaves its despondent, foul
And intractable deposit on its own
    Banks all the way like virtually all

Large rivers, particularly the holy ones, which it
Is not. It sees little that deserves to be undespised.
It only means well in the worst of ways.
    How much of love is much less compromised?

83 *The Clouds*

The craftsmen in my line bred out.
I drive, but could I mend a fuse.
My fathers handled founts of words
My brain would catch and fingers lose.

I find a fair excuse, to serve:
There has, in our society,
Been 'social change', which makes these skills
Much less of a necessity.

83

Beyond your shoulder I can see
A saucer – stamped out by machine –
On the formica shelf near where
We lie on quilts of terylene.

No sort of ancient expertise
Goes to create these modern things:
To them, no craftsman's hand its pride
Or love for their completeness brings.

Their very make and feel rejects
Any thought that such loving powers
Nurtured their shapes to what they are
Through someone's calm and patient hours.

That care seems obsolete. – Yes, I know
You were your parents' artefact,
Your perfect head, shoulders and back
Made in a sort-of skilful act,

But when I move a care-ful hand
(No craftsman's art its legacy)
And dot a pattering line to count
Your poised and tensing vertebrae,

It's not *great* numeracy I want,
Or flair for cold technologies
– Such details are not wanted in
All kinds of loving enterprise.

Nor do we need such skills to lose
All sense of this room, house and street . . .
And don't doubt, though we use no craft,
That love it is makes this complete.

– And, well, on looking up I see,
As a sweet end to summer's drought,
Some wholly unskilled clouds which pour
Blessings of rain on Baron's Court.

84 Comforts

The precisions of idleness:
A ball hit through a hoop on a lawn,
The table-top grained and bare, to which
You take a thin, scrawling pen and paper.
Also, rain is at the green window, scratching.

– Or, posing a record, leaving it
To settle itself, to play;
Or, an immovability about certain white cards
In a shelf-row . . .
Such things, therefore. And, I dare
You, I dare you, disorder.

85 Fortune

Whirling through January, a conclave
Of echoes under a parapet, sleet furring the sheep, and
A cord of salt unthreading onto the table:
        A yellow bell, an orange, a yellow bell.

Circling round April, a syllable scratched in ash,
And flicking past arches on a motorway, though
A white cat waited and washed at the downstairs door:
        A yellow bell, a yellow bell, a peach.

Turning through August, the complexions of two
Terrains various as Iceland and Romania,
Then that important ladder she walked beneath:
        A grapefruit, a yellow bell, a yellow bell.

Spinning in December, and snow spinning, and her
Feet drawn in close on a tall chair, when
Somehow the mirror fled her superstitious hand
        – Three lots of grapes in mauve, ironical clusters!

Shadow containing all shades, glad
Enemy or eluding lover, rabidly
Changeable and sly one, here then
Is the shortest day's tribute, made
In merging, unaccountable images:
Chestnuts fallen on the random
Grass at Hales where the blood once
Lipped the barbaric phial; crude
Skull-bone under a woman's eyes unable
To hide or feign; men wounding
Sweet animals and weeping; music
Becoming phrases becoming music.
                                        Who
Could hold and follow these back to
Say the loose paving stone in the adult
Street this morning, where it
Tripped the crying child? Shadow,
They are yours to understand, and
To repeat; wilted
Wreaths in nightly giving.
                                        Where
Gods are most firm and ancient, you
Are new always, and never certain;
Youthful; a slow, calm hand, or a face
Followed and escaping. Those whom
You love hardly need to dispose limbs,
Or resolve on blankness to invoke you,
But wait merely, only a short time.
Those you despise,
Their bodies char and live in sullen
Fires of wakefulness, quartering and
Rejoining at each chime. Between, lie
All your various supplicants, meditative
Or sad–uneasy, sensing
– So many hundred ways – their
Thoughts meet, link, dissolve into
Illogic, leave consciousness.

                                        Why
        Are you, in whole Valhallas of
        Straight gaze and iron purposings,
        Most sickly and inconstant, working your power
        Through unexpectedness (we never
        See you, but only, ever, wake
        To know that you have passed)?
        You stay invisible; and yet, last night,
        Ruining and re-begetting, you
        Came without terror or long delay,
        Your footfall unhurried, your words
        Kindly and sure, telling no lie, and
        Your arms folding round without
        An ambiguous glance, and you were clear and
        Quick, as petals quivering in daylight.

87 *Somehow*

        The North Lancashire Ballet Group is coming
        Next month, and Miriam Granger-White is giving
        A Francis Thompson reading in the Public
        Library. So we are all well catered for, culture-wise,
        And don't really miss London. It's interesting
        How many talented people do in fact
        Choose the provinces: you seem to get
        Room to breathe here somehow, and so many

        Advantages (for instance, the post for London
        Goes as late as *eleven* on weekdays!). We have these
        Musician friends – the husband's often having things
        Done by the choir of Radio Chesterfield, the wife
        Lectures in a College of Education – they're like us,
        They gave up London because it just didn't seem
        To offer the scope somehow. Robert's work is
        Going awfully well; as I think I told you, it's

                                87

An open-minded, progressive sort of firm, and he has
The chance to do a small, quite modern, country
Cottage for a retired solicitor. He's pretty sure
The standard is as high as a lot of firms
In London. I do several hours each week
Helping at the Family Planning Clinic, there's plenty
To occupy us. Yes, we keep in touch, we can
Get most of our old friends on S.T.D.,

And people really do exaggerate about the northern
Weather. I wouldn't at all like to have
To drive the Anglia in London traffic. I don't think
I could. There's a design shop in the Market Square
Where you can get almost anything, a delicatessen
With every kind of bread we like, and
A fabric shop as good as Oxford Street. Robert
Is on the Third Programme Listeners' Panel.

We are growing lobelias for the local Help the Depressives
Flower Show, which keeps us busy. It's
A good life. Would you like to come down?
We have an enormous spare room and it would
Be lovely to see you. You could stay as long as
You like – we wouldn't bother you. It's
Quite possible, don't you think, to be 'provincial'
While actually living in the metropolis? Anyway,

Write soon, tell us your news, love to Amanda.

As I drove,
to see what
came I was
looking in
the driving
mirror and
saw Aman-
da's face glazed
at air, at
some turn of
the talk. This
was danger . . .
Switch the talk
to something
else, quickly,
please.
               It switched.
We ran up
between two
hedges of
spurting flowers,
the soft clouds
flocked above
to the sun,
quite a fine
afternoon.
I smoked.
               Three
people in
this car in
a country
trip to a
— a house: so
obvious,
easy and
Amanda's
eyes clear now.

Yet I still
saw it there,
another
closing face
seen elsewhere,
with its own
purposed kind
of rigid
calm, and blank
light; and guessed
the intent
look it had
was someone's

very mad.

89 *Peter Daines at a Party*

Oliver Cromwell and Beethoven both
Died in the middle of thunderstorms. Ruth
Didn't know this, but knew Kierkegaard's Dad
Cursed God from a hilltop, or so it was said.
Yet none of these things was at all familiar
To Mary, or Nora, or Helen, or Pamela.

But Pamela knew of some laws of Justinian's,
Helen listened to Schutz and had read *The Virginians*,
And Nora and Mary liked Wallace Stevens,
So in general terms it worked out evens
– Except that none of them, only Amanda,
Knew that Oliver Cromwell had died during thunder.

Still, here were these women with items of knowledge
Picked up in one and another college
– And here am I with not quite all their gaps
In my knowledge of all these high-powered chaps,
Doing well with the female population
And their limited but charming conversation.

90 *Sestina in Memoriam Vernon Watkins*

When, that October, he was at Attingham, I first
Saw him in the early evening: treading with a good
Relaxed stride down the kitchen garden, only to then
Pause under a little brick archway and wonder
If there were really time for a walk before supper, and at last
Turn back, avoiding the rain, to the great

House, to unpack instead.
                              Out of a great
Metal trunk lashed up with ropes, he took first
His poems and notes, then some very orderly clothes, and, at the
    last
Moment, nearly missing the meal, needing to be a 'good
Listener', on the stairs, to a lady full of wonder
At the naturalness of a famous poet, he ate his roast beef, then

Signed a few copies of *Affinities* over coffee, then
Told precise, nostalgic anecdotes of the last
Time he encountered Dylan Thomas; stopping to wonder
How it was he never somehow got beyond the first
Shots at teaching him to drive, on Pendine Sands.
                                          Though good
For several more hours' talk, we did at last

Wander off in search of our respective rooms, the last
People to go to bed; but not knowing where we were, then
Had to grope our way, lost, through innumerable great
State-rooms of irreplaceable relics, probably a good
Half-mile from the room where we first
Sat – and were finally caught up by the Warden, starting to
    wonder

Who it was prowling about . . . I do wonder
Why, when most men drop *two* shoes on the floor above, the last
I heard of Vernon Watkins that night was his dropping first
One, then a second, then a *third* . . . It must have then
Been well past two . . . But he was up early working on a great
Pile of other people's verses, which he covered with neat good

Advice; and at eleven gave his Yeats memorial poem, a good
One to finish with, a fine bardic rendering, from a lectern. I
    wonder,
Still, how his taxi got him to the station in time: it could be, great
And mysterious assistance saved him, in this last
Frantic departure . . .
                        Still . . .
                                    Mere irrelevant scraps? But then
He had this sort-of quality – no one's first

Virtue, and not *his* first, but one power his good-ness had,
Then as always: to give all quirks and details a sort of odd
    wonder,
Each last, least, great thing asking wry gratitudes.

Straight north across Norfolk, the lanes
Lead on past shrines and staithes to assuage
All thirst for greenness and lucidity,
And present at last the Meals and Bights of
An exhausted, exalted coast.
                                    And there start
The contradictions. The spring tide in April is
No resurrection of crested energies, but
A cagey, persistent ripple towards us
Under ghost sunlight, quietly
Marooning the yellowed freshes. Boards
Painted with warnings compromise the apparent
Calm of a sea you could walk into
For placid furlongs. It doesn't feel right, but
Here there seems nothing in the world except
Paradox, any more; and to
Wake after afternoon sleep is a
Reincarnation to the inconsistency of
One's existing at all with this archaic flesh,
Combining, like this place, such aged
And such fervent weathers.
                                    Inland,
The mills casually circle, the cattle
Diffuse in an amiable way over
Ample and undulant clovers, and
The land is quite logically patterned
And fruitful. The silences there
Add layer on layer to themselves, in
Immense stage pauses; disquieting, but
A less ambiguous peace than the sky's
White wideness here over these ancient,
Incredible sandgrains.

There is nothing on
This coast at all comfortable: even inconse-
Quential things are ominous with a hint
Of the not-to-be-explained: little metal
Grids in the water, abandoned
Clothes in the dunes, a quick wheeling-
Off of birds for no detectable
Reason.
And unless you love them, this
Many antitheses would amount in an hour
To a request to go elsewhere; which
We, at least, did not obey until,
Rising from the reed-cries of love we saw
Five black undrowned sisters of chastity
Receding in the very naked light along
The foam-line, with footsteps arrogantly
Murdering the assoiled sand.
It was
Tribute of a further contradiction, almost
Deserving what we had just quite freely
Taken: the freedom of the place.

92   *Lines for a Birthday*

Born fourth out of five. Mother
Had maxims about sunrise and godly
Demeanours. Father went
Away and it wasn't allowed to . . . She
Made him a 'very famous
Scientist'. Fostered, on various
Homes of indigent Florida,
Calling from the table, 'I'm
Starving!' Swam early. Told
Sister at ten, 'If you let the bath-water
Run on you *there*, it gets
Like you kind-of can't *bear* it . . .'

And lay with her, nights, pretending
It was Elvis. Went to High
School, was once voted
Student 'most likely to succeed'
In the year. Collected a
Pack of girls for constructive
Depravity, sat on a long bonnet
For a boy's camera, proposed
Club colours black and grey, was
Fired and let other leaders
Mess it up latterly. Cheered, danced,
Wrote the club song and found
How all the boys tried making it on
Peppermint tongues and false, sun-
Hot leather in coupés. Ran
From the house when sister could
Nearly have been dying; and blamed
Herself. Looked a long time with
Brother, for a Coleridge, to
Complete themselves. Lost It
In five jerks of a quarterback's
Ass . . . homo ludens . . . he hasn't ever
Married. Saved up for U.C.L.A., nearly
A Republican; Civil Rights
At Berkeley. Stayed Karl's
Flat in the poor quarter – and
Went to Mexico for the first one
(Corner of the avenue: 'Americano?'
'Si!' Christ lifted her away
Through the pentathol). Good grades,
Naturally, and surfed on the beaches;
Broke down about obsessions with
Filling, every, single, moment . . . met
With Joe Missile, that being
The second time: a phone call to the flat. 'Say,
Did you get your . . .?' 'No.' Done in
San Diego. Crying in a
Waiting room, yet bored by
Comforting in only six weeks,

Went six
Thousand miles, married, carried
Her mother's admonitions. Adopted
Cats, put down a mortgage, was
Pursued across rooms with knives.
Ate and ate and spoke about it,
Invented William and Rosemary, covers
For lovers. Recalled how
Last summer started working the
Harmless fantasies: Greeks, Finns,
Admirers, haters, blackmailers, mechanics,
Lecturers; had thought to let in
Some of all the professions that . . .
Left, for her own flat; found
The tap in the *centre* of the bathroom wall,
Had 'waited all my life for such a tap – but
The water was ice-cold!'
Taught some people, wrote an exercise,
Lived in a station, lay with this
Frenchman, Saturday, above
Knightsbridge. Today
Cut her forearms in unimportant
Places over the sink, writes, 'Leave
Me, forgive me, this
Is the tomorrow I have chosen, the
Suicide it will mean.' And now the white
Sun rises as we drive south, with
The power-station ambiguously
Applauding, and
Tomorrow is happy
Birthday, Lauren, happy
Birthday, Lauren, happy
Birthday.

93 *Ballad for a Birthday*

I cleaned up the house, and moved the telephone;
I had a look to see if the plant had grown;
I put Tiddles outside, and sat on my own:
    I feel the same, but I wouldn't want to call it love.

I arranged my dresses on laundry hooks;
I pulled out the table and set out my books;
I went to the window for just one or two looks:
    I feel the same, but I wouldn't want to call it love.

I wanted coffee, so I marked the page;
It should have been over when it got to this stage;
Can I *be* the same girl at a different age?
    I feel the same, but I wouldn't want to call it love.

What if he phoned, and I heard the bell
With my feet on the bath-tap, and I couldn't tell . . .
Well, I heard it . . . should I answer it as well?
    I feel the same, but I wouldn't want to call it love.

If he wrote a letter, saying Could we meet,
Or if we met by accident, in the street
— When something's finished, is it *always* complete?
    I feel the same, but I wouldn't want to call it love.

If he drove round here and knocked on the door,
Would I answer his questions, let him ask me more,
Or could I tell him I was absolutely sure . . .?
    — Oh, I feel the same, but I wouldn't want to *call* it love.

In the room,
In the woman's hand as she turns
Is the packet of salt.

On the packet is a picture of a
Woman turning,
With a packet in her hand.

When the woman in the room com-
Pletes her turning, she
Puts the packet down and leaves.

On the packet in the picture
Is: a picture of a woman
Turning, with a packet in her hand.

On this packet is a picture: of a woman,
Turning, with a packet in her hand.
On this packet is no picture

– It is a tiny blank.
                    And now the man waits,
And waits: two-thirty, seven-thirty,
Twelve.

At twelve he lays the packet on its side
And draws, in the last packet in the last
Picture, a tiny woman turning.

And then he locks the door,
And switches off the bedside lamp,
And among the grains of salt he goes to sleep.

95 *Ode to Melancholy*

(for Martin Bell)

I have made England
almost
unusable with associations. Every

beach, square, terrace or
shattered chancel has its
touchy girl, saying

'Don't go back *there.*'
                              So
on Bank Holiday I walk
home, home in the sun. Little

cats jump their heads into
my hand, but I can't talk
to *people.* Closing

my door, it's eight hours
playing and refining the
games of melancholia:

cushions, records,
crumbling sugar-heaps,
self-love. O gentle, helpful

melancholy, give me
one good doodle on a
white page for

all my afternoon's journey;
rescind time's
importance for me so I don't

care how the days of the week are
seven, the days of the month are
seven plus twenty-one; and

feed me black coffee, black
cigarettes, black socks
(toujours

la délicatesse!) – that I can
wait so happily for
darkness to require

all those curtains to be pulled.

96 *White Night*

I did not dream it, no I *was*
A t.v. screen left on shining, and
Insensately vibrating, and
Blank, in a shop at night: like a
Flat yet restless pool.

I could picture nothing; but
I was alive and was shivering and
Wanting to hold more and think more
Than grey, sudden flecks and bleak dots
Momently repeating.

O nice insomnia, fastidiously
Beckoning the abrasive dawn, and tuning
The mind to that first, drab
Water-table where, out of such cold depths,
    came
Monsters on which the hurtful body rode.

The man rummages the intonations of her voice.
He wonders if she will proffer the cigarette.
The filament of the fire clicks once.

She rises with the cigarettes pointing.
She goes to the second woman first, who refuses.
The lights flicker as if his eye had blinked.

She goes to the second man second:
He accepts. She goes back poising her own cigarette.
The draught teems at the stopped-up door.

From her chair she offers now the first man
A cigarette. He takes it quickly, and nods.
A spray of rain patters the reflecting glass.

It is not that they speak. The first man leans
Rapidly to the matches on the table, strikes one.
The clouds of the night outside shift among themselves.

He lights the woman's cigarette, the second man's,
And then his own; relapses eagerly to his chair.
A pitiable vain wind hawks the marshes in darkness.

98   *Projection*

And that midnight raced across
Down the sand, James Carra first. And
Though the air drenched his eyes,
Suddenly he saw the thing, the figure, his
Own shadow running terribly forwards onto

Him, out of the water; because all these four
People were running straight down the
Headlight path in the dark to the shallow
Sea, and had met their ghosts rearing
Up from the tide-edge. Where

The water stood them, the four stood
In quiet and disquiet, trying to trace
The invisible lip of the retrenching
Tide. The sea was unseizably dark.
This distance, the car lights couldn't

Choose out one wave-crest; but then the water
Was blankly calm where the four
Stopped, and couldn't speak, before
Their huge grey shapes hovering
And diffusing upon the Atlantic. Such

Ghosts they were content to own,
Knowing their nature, the un-
Measurable powerlessness of shadows. And when
They turned back up their glaring track
Those vast greynesses comfortingly

Dwindled again (slowly, because they walked)
Dwindled into the sea again, that did
Nothing. Only James Carra, walking,
Thought more than this, as he measured out the
Dark sand and caught at his disrupted breath

– As he knew she would catch, who
Lay across the water in the
Drowning sheets, checking her
Breath for a lover on whom no
Writs or shadows he could cast could run.

99 *Connection*

The first take was an offer in eagerness,
With every white finger so quickly threading,
Those hands went on as if they didn't think.

But they thought for the second take; which was
A slow agreed advancing, and a
Watching with eyes to see what eyes would tell.

The third take was from longer forethought, becoming
A turmoil and grating of little, decorated
Bones; neither hand wanted it.
                                            In fact,

The fourth take might never have been at all,
Except . . . . some kind of separateness travelled
The arm to the shoulder, the shoulder to the brain

And there it spoke: to separate, such hands
Needed to have been joined
                                   and been confused

– Once more those fingers did as they were used.

100 *Crabwise*

                    Sea-crabs live in
                    And near the sea,
                    Land-crabs go back
                    Occasionally.

After these many months the old crab was out of the water,
And into the full, blank air and wanting the sun.

A crab has a very strange
Sideways walk
And eyes placed on
A retracting stalk.

Wide sheets of wet light covered the level beach
As he came fumbling and peering over the gnarled sand.

Two kinds of bodies
For crabs there are:
The oval and
The triangular.

His ten legs carried his squat bulk grave-
ly and slowly like a burden altogether too sad to keep long.

A little crab only
Really begins
To be adult when he's
Cast five skins.

This was his last stroll of years out of the bitter flow and
Hard swirl of the winter water, dragging from pool to clear pool.

A crab's feet are not
All the same, because
Some are for walking
And some have jaws.

His old mouths muttered on the windy silence as he walked.
In his funny clumsiness and misery he was man-like.

When all these men and
women came, in
the sunlight, to that
                    tower they
found it
was embedded
in the earth. And
to get inside, you
crossed over this
iron bridge, to meet
spiralling
                    downward
steps;
which they did,
and proceeded down
-stairs to a room
with only a
white
telephone in it and one
window looking out at hills
barely holding back the sea.
And when the
telephone immediately
                    rang,
a voice told them
don't
go, whatever
else you do, out
by the middle stair
-case door if the
                    horse
is standing in the field with
tresses of blood-wet
silk at its mouth.
How then to
                    get away,
all these lovers and friends,

because when
they
                    opened that door,
they saw, in blank fright,
the enormous horse
waiting
                    and looking
and waiting,
and they must not, could
not go out. Still,
at the top of the spiral of
steps, it was a
hundred fears worse:
a darkening
field of
broken
inscribed
                    graves, which moved
and edged to
-wards them,
and utterly white
funerary
                    statues,
embracing.
At that top door, they
held one
another tightly, but
                    who,
when they looked,
exactly
                    who
were their friends?
Because one by
one, everyone
                    not
thoroughly true to her,
or to himself,
or to herself,
was irrevocably
                    dissolving,

and it was starting to
be, very suddenly,
                    night.
It was so
                    black now, they
couldn't even make out
which of each other's
faces
were still
truly
                    there,
in which fear,
she, and they, tried
hard (it was so
hard now) to breathe, and tried
to speak, and tried to
think how possible in any
-thing like this, any
-thing like
                    dawn
actually

was.

102 *In a Convent Garden*

In the convent vegetable garden the nuns
Have erected a scarecrow in front of the runner beans,
And it has an old wimple on its head.

In the spring the beans will climb, will climb
But the crows are coming:
The wimple will chase them away.

In the convent vegetable garden the nuns
Have erected a scarecrow alongside the cauliflowers,
And it has an old wimple on its head.

In the spring the cauliflowers will rise, will rise
But the daws are deadly:
The wimple will drive them away.

In the convent vegetable garden the nuns
Have erected a scarecrow behind the marrow plants,
And it has an old wimple on its head.

In the spring the marrows will expand will expand
But the tits are terrible:
The wimple will turn them away.

In the summer the marrows will fructify completely,
And will be scrubbed under rubber-nozzled taps and peeled
And sliced and cored and mutton shoved inside

And the scarecrow will be taken apart
And at the long tables in the cool refectory
The Mother Superior and the nuns and the novice nuns
        and the symbolists will sit and stuff
           themselves for a considerable
             length of time.

103 *Palindrome*

We used to be some self-absorbed people living
In a compromised age about twenty years ago. We hated it, it
Was a terrible age, and underneath we liked it in a way, it
    Was because it gave us the chance to feel like that.

Now it has all changed, and we are older,
And we hate the age completely, not nearly so
Entranced with our hatred. But now there are lots of younger
    People entranced with hatred of this terrible age,

While underneath they like it in a way, because
It gives them the chance to feel like that. We ourselves feel lost
Because we can't tell them they are compromised like us,
    That being hard for the self-absorbed to see.

    And all the time the ages are getting worse and worse.

104 *Formosavej*

The tramway ran out along into the night,
Its rails were wet from the rain and the tramway continued.
It met houses, it met shops, it met parks, it met cafés,
It met dogs.

    And in the shining of
The light of the lamps in the rain on its tracks
It went steadily on with its own quiet, metal
Wilfulness all the time.

    On it, the brittle
Narrow, bright, single-decker trams rang and
Rattled: busy and green-grey frameworks
Of glitter and rightness.

    At the many turns
In the wide streets and the by-streets their
Brakes drew in breath and groaned, at
Jolts and bumps on the track all the dainty
Lights went off and came on again.

    Overhead, through all this,
The wires droned and thudded and crackled
And at sudden halts all the empty red-leather
Seats reversed themselves.

When the terminus came,
It was a splendid aggregation of trams on
The circle of tracks at the end of the route,
A stupefying, fascinating, memorable
                    Clatter of numbers

And lights and signs and conductors and drivers
And cheerful spitting sparks at the knots
In the overhead wires. Readers, you would have
                    Enjoyed this as much as I did.

1970s

Two by two this Saturday you little animals
Step with your decoration of hymns and flowers in-
To your waiting compounds; taking your place among all
The ancient objects of living, those graceless
Gifts that will stick for years, like burrs out of reach;
There being, always:
                            Blankets to cover you,
Curtains to curtain you, clocks that will thread your
Disquieted sleeps with duty, and sets of knives.
In all South London a misted orange heaven
Haloes the nurtured hair and suits of smiles.

But in some other uncertain sunlight, of a bad dream,
Such things may rise like some
Sortilegious army, shuddering the compounds,
Greedy to seize their own power and
Wailing in rancour: Can you depart us,
Dismiss us, divide us? – And will need to be
Put down somehow in baskets and sacks
And cases and bags and pockets and
Arranged elsewhere, in a place where they can always be
                seen,
With snarls that stay on their faces until you die.

'When the Saracens overran the shrine at Jerusalem the monks of
Little Walsingham announced that the spirit of the Blessed Virgin
Mary had taken up residence there . . . the resulting flow of pilgrims
brought great wealth to the monastery. . . . Early in his reign Henry
VIII walked barefoot to Walsingham to pay homage. . . . Later, at
the dissolution of the monasteries, the image of Our Lady was taken
to Smithfield and burnt there. . . . The Walsingham shrine is again
today a flourishing resort of pilgrims.'

Norfolk guide-book.

Our Blessed Lady who
Dwelt in the Holy Land
Rose from her shrine that was
Soiled by the heathen hand,

Soared from that martyred place,
Ransacked Jerusalem,
And for her dwelling chose
Our Little Walsingham
Ave Maria

Then every godly soul
Who would make offering
Unto the holy name
To our new shrine did bring

Alms and ten thousand prayers
For her sweet charity,
So that her presence here
Made us prosperity
Deo gratias

One of that long array,
In cruel barefootedness,
Great Henry came this way
To give, pray and confess.

Walking, a pilgrim, with
Hosed and shoon courtiers he
Tore his royal feet on hard
Stones to our monastery
                    In nomine Dei

Suppliant and penitent,
Asking her mercy for
All the sin covered by
The majesty he wore,

Henry bowed down his height
Under her image here,
Many an hour bowed down
In holy pain and fear
                    Miserere nobis

All who attended him,
On reverential knee
Fell at his ordering,
Prayed there as long as he,

Then when he rose and stood,
Promised with him to bear
To us and Her always
Tributes of gold and prayer
                    To help our holy work

Great Henry went; and was
Cursed of our Heavenly King
For the vile mind he showed
In lustful wandering,

And, for the gold he gave,
This way again he came
Bringing for penitence
Edict and sword and flame
                    Instead of naked souls

He who was holy once,
Festering with vanity
Thrust his royal power into
Filth and carnality,

Pillaged our golden shrine,
Taking the Image there
To burn in heretic
Fire at a Smithfield fair
                    No better than a Saracen

Great God is just upon
Avarice and lechery:
King Henry died in grief,
Stricken his treasury,

Useless his proud decrees
Who in sin plunged his . . . head,
Heresy earnt him the
Pox on his dying bed
                    No more than he deserved

Now again in that spot
Glows our new modern shrine,
And pilgrims render their
Gifts to the Form Divine;

In painted village shops
Priests sell on holy days
Pictures and statues and
Rosaries in her praise
                    Who gave us all we have

Thus has God's wisdom done
Justice on princes' sin,
And his strong love made gold
Where dross had entered in:

Where shop and shrine lay de-
Cayed under godless feet,
Sweet truth and goodness fills
All the teeth of the street.
                    Amen

107 *Engagements in Armour*

'For the first time did I engage in armour,
which I found but a dull satisfaction.'
                    Boswell's London Journal

I think they hardly happen any more.
But once, the mettle used to go on with
Such subtle forethought as was a pleasure
In itself: happy cumbrances, sweet slow
Anointments to give safety in the joust.

The tourney was more honourable then!
Little was quite so quickly gained as now,
And yes, there were some kinds of gallantries
Peculiar to the garb. . . .
                    But now, to wear
(Half-way, or more, through your warrior's career)

Nothing but naked ease, this disconcerts.
You feel you need a ritual to mask
The lack of mystery in the mystery,
Some few pretences round it all to hide
The mawkish fundamentals of the war.

Or else it gets to be a woman's thing.

A soured mellowness creeps into the light
After the start of July; because
The best of summer is just about now
Worked through, and the evenings seem resigned
To the season having already lost out.
These short fierce stalks are all
That's left in the shorn fields, with someone's
        hay harvest
Reeking off towards the barns. And my
Birthday comes around the middle of all this,

Arriving just past the place when
The marvels assumed of midsummer are dreamt of
As having lain, somewhere untraceable, back,
A little way back, under wet June days; being
There if one only could really have known.
My birthday is therefore a case of thinking
What was it that could have been worth it, if it
Had not unnoticeably gone? The day itself
Inserts a chill under the August sweat,

Especially towards nightfall, especially towards
This time of life; and stands to summer
As the next circle out stands to the bull on
A target: each approximate hit is challenging
Me back to try for summer again. So that
I feel death's final supervening might come
Like a hand holding back the arm which draws,
Still hopefully, the bow; while my voice, thin, and
        just not
Natural any more, is screaming – 'Look, I've only
        just *begun!*'

Is a lady of twenty-nine in a
Green, neat tailor-made two-piece, a
White collar, tortoiseshell spectacles and
A smooth skin nourished with the pallor of the Court.

There is a cool one, you say, and are right:
It's in the swift, sleek balance of the wrists
Over the documents, and the voice
(Of the deputy senior prefect of
Her public school) that whispers all day so
Accurate a continual
Transcript of proceedings into
A small white mike.

One dull Tuesday, the sort of day that
Can hardly lift its head to speak its name,
I saw her; from the public seats, thank god.
As usual, the sick with power were busy
Afflicting the sad with none, and she
Was in on this, as she would have to be.

I thought she had a stare might disinfect
Whole seas of toxins.

Part of the time she read the charges out.
Part of the time she jotted little notes.
Her fountain pen was a Parker Duofold.

At the end of
a line of
good, elderly squires
came
this last one,
            geared
to the forces of change,
Master of Foxhounds
but also
graduate of Surrey
(honours
in Business Studies)
and a collector of wines
– who one day
called in his
sharpest tenant-farmer
and his best
shepherd from the
slopes of the dale
            and *his*
smartest
sheepdogs, Rover and
Gyp,
            supreme at
heading
the woolly drop-outs off
– and showed them all
a letter and a
newspaper report;
their valley having
suddenly
become measurable
in terms of a
            capacity
of a different sort from
rearing
sheep.

120

Because where
conurban
corporations thirsted,
the streams of the mountains
might
       give,
and a full
valley might quench,
and besides the need
was
       paramount
and the squire
quite liked
the idea.
Three years gone,
only ten letters from
affronted Hampstead and
one defused
time-bomb in a
biscuit-tin,
       Gyp
and Rover laze on
the café shores
where the boats
are tethered for
sailing
       on
the reservoir,
the shepherd
stands in charge of the
       tea-urn
or dowses the plastic
cups, the farmer
papers the walls of
the clean new flint
cottage from which
he walks out to
       oversee
the embankments,
and the squire is

addressing a
conference of civil engineers
on 'Landscaping for To-morrow'
at a week-end
                school at
the University of York.
Warm Sundays in summer,
nose-to-tail
in long, loveless
processioning after
what neither
water nor anything
else can provide,
the well-cooled
cars from the conurbation
sidle the new road
to the concreted
edges of the lake,
while back at home
the sprinklers
rotate in solitude
on the lawns of Croft and Mead.

III   *Weeping Doll*

A trapdoor in the pink tin knickers
Of the weeping tin doll set down outside
This chemist's in Notting Hill is
Padlocked, tight, in a little bronze clench.

Open it wide when the key is fetched, and all
Your donations will tumble out, every coin
That activated her high slight wail for
The mortal disease she tells of in

This pitying locality, when you dropped them
Through the slot in her downturned lips.
One need not name the incurable demon (a
Crutch carries one unwithered shoulder

Of this articulate creature) but better celebrate
The goodness of the people spending coins
To make her weep and help her, so she
Lives a little longer on their small change.

Twice a month, a man drives round W.11
To all the dolls, stops his painted van
('The National Society for . . .') and
Unlocks all the knicker-trapdoors and takes away

Pennies and even sixpences to prop
Her twisting bones. This man has children, too,
Works for them as an accountant for a big company,
And does this voluntarily at night

– It keeps the whole thing personal, and he
Is rather proud of fifteen pounds twelve shillings
Taken from seven dolls in just one trip.
                                        A sunlight
No pestering State could hope to intercept

Shines sometimes on this area, where,
Who knows, the very same company may even
Own some of the houses where people try to live
– Enjoying the freedom of their choice to help

Others, and save taxation, and show a lovely
Unforced charity passing by and feeding
The weeping doll with enough stray pennies
To set her wailing many many times a day.

Some pining cows – with unenchanted sniffing –
Browsed the wan grass. Straggles of green wheat lay
Thrown down by ill-conditioned winds near where
A river dragged past, in a surly way.

Between two stony, grubby settlements,
There was a bend in a connecting lane
Providing, helpfully, some pallid verges,
And here the foxhunt met, in spraying rain.

Sound flesh and arteries swelled boldly outwards
Over the confident bones; the usual
Red coats and leather trouserings were sported;
Their little caps were the identical

Hunt gear for anywhere; and each man had
A placid piebald which, as he proudly sat,
Fumed feathery steam from nostrils set in faces
Looking well-pleased to do what they were at.

An indoor lighting, very blue and feeble
– A sort-of paintwork of the high sky-shell –
Fell on the hounds, brought up in snarling batches
And loving it, so far as one could tell.

Then, at a billowing horn-call from the master,
Each creature fled off, with a huge sultry bound
After a prey let fly for their pursuing
And chased across a grey and powdery ground.

In all these men and women pride was burning
To have this ceremony in such a place:
The air-locked air smelt grand, the beasts were sprightly,
The clothes were filled with arrogance and grace.

The faces, just as furious and paltry
As were their ancestors' before their births,
Joyed at the springy touch of lunar pastures
As had those solid forebears' on the earth's.

If some forebears had dared to be the first ones,
And radioed back, and from a special bag
Took cameras to photograph each other
And set them up a little national flag,

And gave rehearsed extempore impressions
Of how it felt on their historic day,
And walked around collecting bits and pieces
On screens two hundred thousand miles away,

All this was so that natural human measures
Could dance themselves wherever men might be,
With nothing fine or beautiful neglected,
And nowhere closed to oafish liberty.

113   *Calypso for Sir Bedivere*

But it was not only a sword to me,
It was a symbol, like, of virility.

King Arthur said, 'Take the sword away,
Throw it back into that lake today.'

> *Now King Arthur was a*
> *Wise old king,*
> *But why should he under*
> *-Stand everything?*

So I went down as a loyal knight should
And looked at the lake in an uneasy mood,

And was shaping to throw the sword in the water
When suddenly a very subliminal thought oc-

Curred to me: 'Whoever *wants* to lose
A trusty weapon that is still some use,

'A rational man would want to retain
His faithful tool and use it again,

> King Arthur may be a
> Wise old king,
> But is he tuned in to
> Everything?'

So with this sensible reasoning,
I stashed the sword and went back to the king,

And to change the subject I stood and lied
About the marvellous, marvellous countryside.

But the king said, 'I can quite well see
There are one or two things you are not telling me,

'Go back and throw that sword in the lake,
Tell me what you see, make no mistake.'

> King Arthur was a
> Wise old king,
> But why should he have to guess
> Everything?

Well, a second time I went down to the edge
And took out the sword to fulfil my pledge,

And cast it, for the king, out into that mere,
When suddenly I thought, 'No, I *can't* stand here

And fling this thing into that dirty pool,
It's a work of art, and valuable:

> *King Arthur may be a*
> *Wise old king,*
> *But does he know the cost of*
> *Everything?'*

So another time I went back up along
And told the king how I'd stood there, long

Time gazing at the lovely scenery
– But still he was not believing me.

He said, 'Go back down and take that blade
And throw it in the water just like I said'.

Then I thought:

With the king being terribly stern to me,
Can I prick against the kicks of authority?

So a third time, then, I went down to the brink
And looked at the water, as black as ink,

And picked up the sword (what else could I do?)
And with one strong, well-meaning lunge I threw

It right out *there*.
. . . . There was a clatter and I saw it drop
On the flat of its blade with an almighty plop,

Making little muddy bubbles in the foggy light
As it awkwardly, gradually sank from sight.

> *Well, King Arthur was a*
> *Wise old king,*
> *But he didn't hear the facts*
> *About everything.*

The lake was murky and the light was dim
And I saw no mystical samite limb

Or anything else that I pretended,
And thus when I turned around and wended

My way back up to King Arthur's shrine,
I had to invent things – tell him some fine

Story of how I plucked up courage and then took
A mighty throw, and with a beautiful, incisive
                    look

About it, the sword fell and entered the water
                    clean,
And the smoothest arm I had ever seen

Came up and eagerly clutched it through
Into the silky depths of the evening dew

– It had to be a story, you will surely see,
Fit for a symbol of virility.

>   *But let's come to the*
>   *very revealing point of the*
>   *whole discreditable episode –*

>   *King Arthur was a*
>   *Wise old king*
>   *But he didn't tell the truth*
>   *About everything.*

King Arthur listened while I had my say,
With a gimlet look that gave nothing away,

Then he rose on one elbow and put out one hand
And pretended he could suddenly understand.

And he said: 'Reversing that history,
Yes, exactly the same thing happened to me,

And the way you describe you finally shot it,
That was the way I originally got it:

The arm that came up to grab and take,
Handed it to me out of that lake.'

> King Arthur was a
> Wise old king,
> But no, he didn't tell the truth
> About everything.

And you can blame me and you can blame the king
If you've never done any equivalent thing.

If you've never told some fancy history
To make art cover up for reality.

114 *Ode to Centre Point*

One of the most
Paradoxical of infertil
  -ity symbols
Lately contrived, a vast
  Barren phallus of
Egg-boxes without eggs, it
  Simultaneously wav
-ers and maintains its own
  Projection into the
Soft depths of the sky, a
  Thing of monumental
Insignificance, making no
  Impression and
Quite ignorable, unless for
  Its huge vac
-uity. But in so rapidly
  Appearing, it rased out
Everything lively on its site:
  Small blocks of
Usefully inhabited mansion

Flats, various
Helpful shops, a passable
        Ristorante, an
Experimental theatre, and
        All of the navigable
Pavement on one side of the
        Charing Cross Road,
Substituting, at ground level, a
        Blue pond inside
Crass concrete walls with square
        -Fingered fountains jetting
The water; and above, shooting upward
        A weird, implacable
Cliff of patterned stone, glass and
        Air, a hive of empty
Cells, tilting, apparently, as the
        Clouds above pass over,
And at one dizzying, approximate
        Count, thirty-three stories high.
Therefore, it impinges on us all,
        Notwithstanding, and needs
To be taken into account; which
        Is why strong men with de
-termination and research have
        Gone grey trying to
Discover why it is there
        (But then who, exactly,
Wanted and actually willed Shell
        Mex or the Euston Road?)
−And what it is to do? Such
        A thing is like the
Clothes without the Emperor,
        Flaunting what looks like
Purpose in order to cover weakness
        And chaos, proving again
That somehow, in our time, all
        Towers are peculiarly
Bad, contraptions of anti-sense,
        Contraceptions of truth,
And things which one day might,

With the clarity of simply
Looking at what is there, be just taken
    Down and scrapped. Indeed,
What couldn't we do when even
    The few square yards on
Which we base giant follies were
    Fruitful and even
Innocent again, with perfectly
    Natural weeds? To
Have *this* one as a play-space for
    Technocrats to
Run around and play utterly
    Virginal games of Bank Robbers on,
Instead of the real thing,
    Might be a splendid
Idea for its owner to instal
    If he ever repented
Of the tremendous non-use to which
    He put one quarter
-acre of our possible grass. And
    Perhaps one damn good
Roundabout with small, wry,
    Cynical horses' faces to
Ride on, going perpetually grinning
    Round and round would be,
Though futile, a bit more sense.
                      Mean
    -while, until the world
Turns thus inconceivably pure
    And benevolent, the whole thing
Will rear up in front of the eye,
    Narrowing into the heavens and
Widening at its base like some
    -thing unnatural and
Unmotivated found one morning
    In any man's life, and
Probably the result of some
    Nasty and unremembered
Dream.
    Well, in a way, I'd hate

– With its uniformed toughs, trained
Alsatians and all, to knock it down
    And spoil anyone's happy
Fantasies, an act for which I may
    Have no moral right after
So much indulgence of my own,
    But . . . one's most citizenly
Sort of impatience sometimes rises,
    Just as suddenly, wishing
It lugged with it some uncitizenly
    Substance which might go
Off, and reasoning: Reality ought to be
    -gin somewhere, so why not
With somebody else, who has thirty-two
    Storeys less of it than me?

115 *Ballad of Scarlet and Black*

Waking at her lover's knocking, or
So she thought, she crossed, running,
A carpet twenty yards wide
To the curtains at the window, scarlet-
And-black,
And drew them.

Or so she thought.
                Because
Behind the first curtains were
More curtains, and behind
The second were third,
And behind the third were fourth, none
Of them opening into daylight and onto
Her lover's face waiting at her door,
But onto only
Scarlet-and-black and then
Scarlet-and-black and then
Scarlet-and-black.

But several seconds later truly waking,
She drew
The curtains which were not in her dream,
And were one foot from her bed,
And were scarlet-and-black
And let straight daylight immediately in.

So now she combed, at her mirror, with
Fingers over open eyes, a parting in her hair,
                counting
Which day of daylight this was, and counting
The years of her life again.

And when her lover called, she
Went across town with him talking of her dream
                and what it meant,
Talking of their parting, and joining, and their
                endless counting of time,
And she was trying, trying to uncover
His daylight face.

Up the stairs to his room,
Their blood was the blood of veins returning
                to the heart,
Returning as if with ritual nostalgia
                to the heart,
Between scarlet and black.

There, pulling the black,
Lying under the scarlet, curtains, unhooked
                from the wall,
They made again the love of years,
With his face in darkness;
And then, with fingers across closed eyes
She sorted apart her hair
And slept until the next daylight arrived
                to be counted.

Sadly on barstools, in a city which doesn't speak
English with their accents, two have come together
Of whom one is asking the other advice, very frankly,
About a third – to whom neither is connected
By blood, or sexual ravin: just anxious friends,
And wanting to save Amanda's and William's marriage
                                    because
They prefer it that way.

The drinks, the bar, the barman, the fast bar clock
Are spun away to nothing among a cat's cradle
Of lovely information and speculation: who
Should, for whose future good, intervene
With whom, and if possible when,
And as between Friday in Greenwich or Sunday in
                                    Islington,
It isn't decided yet.

Common citizens unlike them, and more usual in this place,
Are flocking round,
With ordinary drinks that have not seriously, ever,
Strained the cellars of the Bull. The television,
Shoved on the shelf above the forgotten picture
Of part of the local docks in 1910, is showing
A retrospective tribute to Michael Miles.

Wimbledon. Centre Court. Blank and pitiless sun. Many
Eyes misted with, as it were, emotion.

The Old Fox is playing young Kenny Trabner of Australia.
The Old Fox sticks to a baseline game, Trabner is
Up at the net for the volleys, leaning back
At unthinkable angles for the smashes. Cunning,
Age, and experience facing
All the burnished arrogance of youth, Trabner
Playing the ruthless tennis they play now,
And things not going too well at all for the Old Fox.

Trabner, too, in immaculate shorts and Sassoon
Coiffure, the Old Fox, bald, in full-length, pre-war
Flannels, and wearing a green eye-shade on his forehead
Above his bifocals;
But the crowd is on his side.

Can the Old Fox do it this time, *can* the Old Fox do it again?
Things don't look too well. First set
To Trabner, 6–0. Second set
To Trabner, 6–0. It is a crafty tactic the Old Fox is trying.
Third set, Trabner leading 5–0 and 40–0 in the sixth game,
On his own service.
This will need all the Old Fox can pull out, but
Throughout his career the Old Fox has somehow been
Strangely able to pull something out,
So to speak, in moments of crisis.

Now the crowd is utterly still, now the princess
Fingers the Cup, in the Royal Box, with excitement that
                                        mounts weirdly. Trabner
Is serving for the match, three balls bunched
In one broad hand, and
The first ball lifts. And as
The thunderous, upward, apparently final trajectory

Of Trabner's racquet begins, the Old Fox
Pulls out from the pocket of his flannel trousers
An ancient flintlock pistol such as might be hired
For commercial t.v. serials about the Jacobite Rebellion,
And fires.

And Trabner falls. The crowd is on ten thousand delirious,
Cheering, swooning feet. With a last
Expenditure of feeling the princess accidentally shudders the
                                            Cup from its plinth.
The Old Fox leaps the net and shakes Trabner's dying hand.
The newsmen, as they are said to do, crowd round.
The umpire calls out, 'Game, Set, Match and Championship to
                                            the OLD FOX.'

Max Robertson says, 'Yes, the Old Fox has done it again!'

118   *The End*

Not simply human, but all,
But all matter dying there,
Dwindling and tottering away to
A much-more-than-cosmic pit,
An ultimate dark,
An inconceivable collapse:

If so, a tough
Test for the relationship (of matter with
Logic and physical laws)
And as tough for you and me.
But I
Should like to think we could be there, and see:

On the brink of the last collapsar, surviving;
Linking us, ten finger-tips dwindled already
Into two precariously-poising fives.

A touch commemorating all our
Mutual matter's scars from a thousand
Previous little deaths, and falls. Would

We balance, balance,
Humorously on that very final edge
(Such as we often stepped to) smiling
As ever before in that dark, waiting the worst,
Elated in our own, as its, contractions,
Feeling no vortex greater than ourselves?

119　*April Fool's Carol*

Celebrate today belladonna and shot silk.
Women will do what they are for.

Belladonna: poisons in
Certain quantities are a cure.
Women will do what they are for.

Shot silk: it changes at a look, you move
It varies, contrary; but
Is completely one, its feel
Will rub the best and nothing, ever, more.
Women will do what they are for.

The Marys are at every birth, and grave
Delivery, at every marriage too they wear
Their ancient finery: *Women*
('Sing all a green . . .')
                    Will do what they are for.

Thrown out and buried from the colander,
The peelings struck. Potatoes flowered
Blue, white and green,

English republican colours, on
Our wartime flower-beds.
                                    I see
My great-aunt now, thrifty

And foresighted patriot, calendar
Of Winston on the wall, bending
To dig. She grew tomato-plants

And forsook zinnias, she planted out
Saplings of wilted lettuce which would
Hold the invader back; well,

Indirectly. Thus the war years were:
In things like this, a concen-
Tration of particular sensibleness,

A living-on by what would keep
Us living on; not blitzes,
Factory pep-talks, flags on maps,

Not shining uniforms and Alameins,
Or V-signs, tanks and refugees, oh not
That annual stutter of King George VI,

That Churchill-rant – simply making ends meet,
Cutting bread thinly, having
Just enough things to wear, etc., that.

We'll grumble now at imposts on Montrachet . . .
Sometime we'll get perhaps
A commonwealth of sense, and not with guns.

121 *Unnumbered Road*

(for S.L.W.)

She walks in bleeding and smiling from a midnight road/
   she can't remember it/she remembers all of it/
  her hair is black and grey at once/her
hand trembles to be familiar/it is
 calm with its familiarity/her face
   smiles and bleeds/the car turned over twice
   on a road at midday/she can't keep
    her hand from shaking/she can't keep it
shaking/her friends were all there/none of them at all/
   they said her hair was grey and black at once/
her face bled while it smiled/her voice
   talked while it was silent/
  he could understand/she
turns the car over in her head/her
   hand is calm when it trembles in his/
which holds it for the first and hundredth time/
   it is now/it is months ago/the friends have all gone/it
 is night/it is morning/they are all coming back/
    the night is black and grey at the same time/
 the dawn is black and grey at the same time/
    her lips close to open/
it is all calm/it is shaking with strangeness/
   he puts out his arms to hold her for the first time/
    she holds him before he can touch her/
   he turns the car over in his head/
  he turns her body over in his arms/she
is night and dawn at once/she is
    black and grey at once/she is
   smiling in his arms/she
 is bleeding in his arms for the first time/
   for the hundredth time/he is smiling in her arms/
they are calm/they are shaking with strangeness/
   the friends are constantly there having gone away/he
 is constantly there having gone away/he has
    come back from a midnight road

turning over a car in his head/and
she is smiling she is smiling/she is bleeding she is bleeding/
he hears his voice saying her name her name/
they are crying/they are smiling/
it is night/it is dawn/
he has at long last without a second's waiting
temporarily meshed his contradictions
with hers for ever

122 Grey Ground

In the Cornwall wind
I stood with the mine-shaft behind me.
Something said, a toneless kind-of-voice said, 'Don't
Walk on that ground.'

The ground was plain mud and stones, a grey stretch, safe.
But, 'Don't walk on that ground.'
I had flung and heard the pebbles in the dark shaft
Fenced off under the brick stack, black.
Was the grey ground not safe?

The wind worked at the firs' tops,
It had that whisper, 'Don't walk on
That ground.' The pebbles in the shaft
Clanged, and hit echoes. The echoes touched out
Echoes. The echoes said, 'Don't walk on that
Ground.'

The death-shaft gulped and trapped the echoes of the pebbles.
The ground was mud and stones, is mud and stones,
A grey stretch, not fenced off now, thirty years
Safe, still. People have walked on it,
Thirty years.
I did not walk on it when I was ten.

I stand here, thirty years after, in the Cornwall wind,
A man, looking at the grey ground. The firs' tops
Work and whisper.
The day is a clearer day, the sea visible,

The sun is out. A woman touches my arm.
We are standing with the mine-shaft behind us swallowing
Echoes of thirty years ago, of a minute ago,
Pebbles we have both thrown, smiling.

Something says, a toneless kind-of voice says
'Don't walk on that ground.'

123 *In Hertfordshire*

Not very meek are the polytechnics, they
Shall inherit the earth; what there is left
After Construction Units' rummagements. – Come
Hell and the low waters of this stricken place,
I might elude it by transmogrifying to
A cat safe with ninety-nine lives on
A Hemel Hempstead walkway, or a muddied

Reservoir swan, or a magpie fumbling
The scrawny grasses of roadhouse roundabouts,
But this would be enduring, not enjoying:
Single-manned nearby, the Green Lines would
Rattle on, more slowly than the stagecoach, past churned
-up verges stuck with signs, and it would make,
Like other people's, a sort-of country life.

But living, a human in all this, system-built
For profit-sharing, for Helping to Build the Firm,
One would feel all the prep schools, in big Victorian houses
Among arranged glades eking out the hopes
Of the techno-bourgeoisie; dance, young, in the formica
Discothèques of Letchworth; rent house where Ebenezer's paltry
Cities are nailed down in the duckboards of Hatfield; carry

One's young in wire Macfisheries baskets across
Littered precincts of pools and statuary; grow old
In the Community Centre in front of screens pocked with
Supersonic interference; get interred
In somewhere undulant and discreet behind
A subtopian hill. Against all this, in Barnet perhaps,
Some poor bloody Blake might frenzy a while, then

    Take out a mortgage himself, or move to Leeds. – Though
Consumer Groups rampage, and the Hadley Green Fabians
Plan, plan soft turquoise bathrooms in central heating,
And the spirit's life goes on (flocks out
On Sundays of Vivas and Dolomites to wafers and
Lollies of sweet consolation, New English
Sermons and Welwyn's holy ice-cream chimes),

    All around, in securest sunlight, the
Brownies parade for Thinking Day, the Rugby Clubs
Run their Development Sweepstakes, the commuters play
Aryan golf and buy private treatment, and
Telescoped Avengers lie on the reservations among
Sprays of demented glass as company
Jaguars bray, and scream, past.
                       So don't get there if you

    Need not, you'd find your escapable future ready,
                               grazing
With jaws like Corporations on miles of forgotten
Scrub forty miles from the centre of the boil:
It has fangs of reinforced concrete and triple glazing,
Its eyes are huge stacks of strip-light in Industrial Areas
Refining precisions to blur life, imprinting so tidily on
Clicking cards the specific patterns of your death.

I am writing my text-book of modern American history
It will sell in all the schools
Every school will buy fifty dozen copies
One for every child in every class
In a given year
It should appear about 1963
My book will sell in millions
To the school authorities
It will be stored ready
In millions
On the shelves of great depositories full
Of textbooks for schools
My book will make me a fortune
It will have fine clear diagrams
Fine clear expositions
And be a fine text-book yes
The depositories will be full of it
The depositories will be air-conditioned
Men will walk around the depositories in grey coats
Counting and packaging the books
Including my book
They are wonderful places depositories why
You could get lost in depositories or hide
And not be seen for hours
You will be able to get lost even among the copies
Of my book
I will have done a humble service
Publishing my book
I shall be able to say to myself
I could have done innumerable worse things
Than publishing my book
Than helping to fill with books like mine
Depositories so big you could hide and not be found
Now tell me what harm ever came of depositories of books?

First, prolonged and weird estuarial waters,
     And so wide before you realise: full of rusted,
Sunken, purposeless objects; or creaking guide-lights
     Offering unclear channels, curving paths
Of a grey water greyer than the rest. And now the eager
     Sea-birds that followed have dropped back for the shore.
The strip-lighting blinks on in the Dining Room, the cutlery
     Scintillates. But you don't enjoy their small-talk at the
                                                   table, as
The white-coated band on the platform lilts into selections,
     Selections: it's a musical about your life they
Are playing them from, and it could not have run long in
                                                   town.
     Now the ship tilts, and the crockery slides downhill; and
There is a tannoy announcement from the captain:
     Welcoming you to the ship, hoping you will be
Comfortable, and reminding you there is no destination.
     You leave the table for the bar. Already it's dark, which
Might be more interesting; though you expected, looking out,
     That a scattering of stars might show; and the sky's dull.
Far off, is it west, you can pick out an esplanade
     With lights like a frippery of beads; you
Never attained that one, wherever. Your drink hasn't lasted,
     The print in your newspaper blurs and you can't see faces
Very clearly. The map, of the route of the ship in
     The frame on the wall, is practically blank. Is there a rest
                                                   room?
The stewards don't attend to you, they are attending
     To the bed-makers in the cabins. The duty-free shop
Is a shut grille. The handrail in the corridor misses
     Your hand, upstairs both sides of the deck cant you into
The bullets of the spray. The wake is dark, the prow is
                                                   chained off.
     You go to the Engine Room for the monotone of the
                                                   drone,
But that is no anaesthetic. There should be
     Amusements aboard, surely? What about the staterooms

144

Looking so sumptuous in the brochures? And the gilt lounges?
   Something worth having this ticket for? God, this ship feels
No different from being alive; because
   Your seaboard walk shakes like your walk on land, and
All your thinking ends at the same advice: it's time, no
   Other choice, to go down the metal steps to
Where it says Men, and lock the door; be alone, alone,
   You may find, there, what's wrong that you couldn't
Name, that nobody found out.
                                          – So this you do, except
   That when you have closed the door, the door locks
On you. Rust runs in lifelong trickles from the welded
   Bolts of this cubicle; everything shudders, even more,
In you and the whole ship. No hammering for help,
   Or calling, it's H.M.S. Death, death: the eternal
Accumulated store of everything life became: just
   Yourself, as you are, and your face in that bowl. Smile,
                                                              you're free
To vomit your self-regard for the rest of the voyage.

126   *An Elegy on Mademoiselle Claudette*

Mourning the final death from disbelief of one
Who lies now farther out than her rival's sword;
The sea, having had her at last, being
A fit receptacle and outcome. She
Was thirty-two when she died, I having
Given her first credulity when I was eight,

And the ideal reader. Somewhere they met,
Her fatalism, my childhood, and made strange friends:
She held her world with fingertips of ice
On chalices of poison. She was in the eyes
Pulling mine at fifteen over café floors, she stared
Out from trains, she dared in time to come near and be

145

No different, even when she undressed. The spell didn't
Break, because she was always gone next morning,
A skyline figure on horseback, not leaving a note.
And this continued some while, her cloak
Flowed at numberless parties, and she nurtured
Linguistic codes beyond mine, and had flats

(Which I never went to) all mauve lights and white divans,
Acting indestructible enough to be
A life-force in her way, a fuel for one kind
Of imagination. But what could she keep when
Life coarsened, and truth walked in? Well,
She thrived for a while by updating her devices,

Like – playing the metropolis, all the sleights of
Communications, the trick of the very new:
She was good at sudden taxis, away, in the small hours,
Had a dreadful skill with things like the letter
Never sent because of the promise to phone,
Never kept. And she had this vague gallery of

'Friends' to refer to, in a sensual, significant abstract,
No names vouchsafed. She was trying hard, was desperately
Applying the cosmetics of decline. – But she's
Abstract herself now; finally dead; not
Struck down by some other in contest, not replaced
By odder enchantments, not vanquished by any

Conversion from Snow Queens to Earth Mothers, none
Of that: she just couldn't keep up the pose.
It was not so long back that her last departure
Took place. She put out one entreating hand in velvet,
But it looked like something ghost-written for her.
I tried to feed those plaintive metaphors, I searched

The depths of my compassionate soul for faith
To keep her alive; but all the same she died.
And sad the way daylight lastly saw her sink,
Poor Mademoiselle Claudette: leaving shadows of stances only,
Vague rags of garments, tawdry stage properties,
And terribly dry pink tissues on bedroom floors.

My dancing is, in my opinion, good,
In the right, cramped circumstances, and provided
Other people are too preoccupied with
Their own to notice mine. I am happy
To have lived into an informal age when
Standing and shaking in approximate rhythm, not
Bowing and guiding, is the idea. Because to
Have to know regulated steps and be skilful was what
I could never manage at all when it was the thing.

So I do dance. But I'm never entirely sure.
It's a kind of movement you would never make
In the normal course, and how much it always seems
To obtrude on the natural in an embarrassing
Way wherever people get it started!
Set it apart, on a stage, with a large
Orchestra, it's all right, it's undoubtedly clever,
And the costumes are glorious to gawp at, but
It still looks a little bit foolish, moving like *that?*

To speak of how all its origins are so
Utterly primal – the planets, the seasons,
The rhythms of mating, and so on, and so on,
Is to list a lot of fundamental things,
Explain them, and exorcise dancing:
Because simply why dance if you've come to understand
What dancing mimes so roughly, or makes such
A repetitive pantomime of? Sleights of courtship,
Postures of delight, grief, vanity, idolatry I see

All around me more sharp and subtle for not being
Done in a style. Dancing has social uses,
I know, but so did elemental spears and punches before
They invented tables for eating and conducting
Verbal negotiation (and does hands
Gripping slyly under a table ever happen
In the middle of a fandango?)
Moreover, if the elemental stuff
Of dancing is banal, the ancient, ritual and customary

Panoply of 'the dance' is incredibly peculiar:
Fellows in feathers, or kilts, or puma-skins,
Guys trinkling little bells down there in Hampshire,
Or folding arms over black boots flicking in the
Urals . . . one surely turns away to find somewhere quieter,
Where one needn't be part of a silly circle
Of grins, clapping hands in moronic unison (I once
Took a pocket torch in, to go on reading – *The Listener*,
I believe – all the way through a Gene Kelly musical).

For ostensible moralist reasons, the
Puritans disliked dancing: but they also
Opposed all giving and wearing of jewellery,
In which they may well have been right; so with dancing,
They may also have come at the truth
From a wrong, religious direction. But, down Oxford Street
These days, whatever the mortgage rate, there jogs
In shine or rain an irrelevant group of chanters
Shuffling to the rhythm of tiny cymbals, opposing

Shaven sublimity to the big, crude, selling
Metropolis around; and *dancing*, in sandals, for converts.
They'd like to see everyone join them . . . how unlikely,
I think; and how such unlikelihood shows
That most of us only don or discard our
Finery, to dance, in a fit of social desperation.
I recall that outside the Hammersmith Palais,
There once was an illuminated sign announcing
A group of performers known as THE SANDS OF TIME.

For months, the words, I surmised, were a motto
Of that establishment: a thousand grains shaken
Nightly in that vast box, a thousand softies
Sifting for life-partners as the hours and days
Ticked on in tawdry, implacable rhythms. Yet the
Dancing prospers – telling how many the world leaves
Despoiled of words, of gestures diverse and specific,
Of shades of forehead, or hintings of finger-tips,
Or any more delicate tremor that speaks the whole thing;

And this is the crux. Tides vary, exact shelvings
Of pebbles on shores don't repeat, while patterns of clouds
Are never the same, are never *patterns*. Raindrops,
At unforeseen moments run, and weigh, down, minutely,
A million particular grass-blades: movement, movement,
Everlastingly novel shifts of a universe not
Gracelessly ordered, not presided by a setter of
Regulations. Vanity is so sad pretending to represent
Nature with humans dancing. Those who can move need not
dance.

128 *Negotiation*

In the same post, the Old Fox receives
Word that he is in overdraft at the bank,
And a gas bill for £3.69.

Ten days later, the Gas Board write again, in red, 'They would
Be grateful if . . .' The Old Fox waits.

Two weeks later, the Gas Board write, in red again, some
Phrases underlined, 'Regret, you do not tender payment with-
in
Seven days, supply disconnected, charge for re-connection.'
The Accounts Officer's signature is stamped below.

Six days later, the Old Fox carefully writes a letter:
'Thank you for, apologies for any inconvenience,
Do not wish cause difficulty, wonder if payment
Of sum outstanding *by instalments*, very grateful, Yours etc.'

A week having passed,
Drinking coffee made on his undisconnected cooker,
The Old Fox reads, 'Must regretfully state, not customary,
Payment by instalments when sum entailed so small,
No alternative but to ask, within five days,
Supply disconnected unless, Dictated by the Accounts Officer
And signed in his absence . . .'

Four days passing, the Old Fox writes, 'Thank you courteous
                                                    reply,
Recollect (which is untrue) kindly permitting me
Payment by instalments, previous occasion, some years ago,
Comparable sum, possibly consult your records, appreciate
Your looking into this, regret any delay caused,
Only anxious to settle account as soon as possible.'

The Gas Board writes after a week, ignoring this.
'Supply disconnected unless . . .' The Old Fox rejoins,
'May I direct your kind attention, my letter of,
Possibly held up in the post, possibly crossed with yours of,
Sorry to put you to this, Yours etc.'

'We have looked into our records,' the Gas Board two weeks
                                                    later,
'Can find no precedent in your case, not our custom with
                                                    small amounts,
Must insist on immediate settlement, otherwise steps
Will be taken, supply disconnected, recovery of sum
By legal action, Yours very truly, Accounts Officer'
– Personally signed.

Sadly, then, the Old Fox writes a cheque for £3.69,
Omits (on purpose) to sign it,
And posts it to the Board.

In eight days, the cheque is returned, 'For your signature,
Yours truly.' The Old Fox waits.

A month later, 'We do not appear to have received cheque
On which your signature was requested, bring this
To your kind attention.'

It is winter by now, and the gas fire gleams.
The North Sea roars on the cooker to heat
The Old Fox his supper of Irish stew from a tin.
Lighting his gas water-heater, he runs a bath.
It mellows him. He writes his name at the bottom of the
cheque
(Which will come back 'referred to drawer' in nine days'
time.)

Returning from the pillar box, he picks up the next quarter's
invoice from the mat.

129 *Letter to America*

I take a long lick of this envelope,
Getting an unsweet, unAmerican taste:
The glue of England, which does not pretend.

The middle-classes drink precisely
From the far side of the other person's cup,
But kiss more deeply than the workers do

– Say sociologists. One day, we parked outside
A backstreet house in Wandsworth, kissing
In just that way, not thinking of social class,

And this in broad daylight, very visibly,
When an aproned lady came out quite displeased,
And motioned to us, literally shaking

Her hand with her wrist as if her hand
Were shaking a duster, wanting us to move on.
The moral disapproval was very clear.

And the point is, do you remember this at all,
Which came to me as I began to lick
Your envelope? Since, if you don't recall,

Invisible dust, from a hand shaking it, may
Have settled on us and on the whole Atlantic
– Covering also what this letter means.

And need I have unsealed it to say all this?

130 *Old Nightwork*

Shallow: And is Jane Nightwork alive? . . . certain
she's old, and had Robin Nightwork by old Nightwork
before I came to Clement's Inn. *(Henry IV Part 2)*

1
Loathing the day-, if not the candle-, light,
Old Nightwork burrows by unsocial hours,
Preferring heavy curtains: velvet pelts,
And under them, so warm to sooth and seethe.

2
By definition working by darkness,
Nightwork can freely imagine it is anyone
Provided she is of average shape and size
Assuming she is not much different in behaviour
Given that she stays silent
As long as his head is not plagued with associations
Granted the place is anonymous and dark

And until his eyes grow used to the dark.

3
This epitaph for British Standard Time,
So hatefully abrupted in its prime:
Let it lie, if it must, in peaceful rest,
This kindly scheme, which succoured the depressed
By giving them at dusk a longer day,
And in the morning holding dawn away
For one sweet hour.
               Soon may it come again
To help Old Nightwork and his screwed-up Jane.

4
Love as light being a figment of chastity,
Nightwork keeps, as a brief lamp, only
The after-image of the crass filament
On his eyeballs: all senses then are bent
On the tactile patterns of the blackness,
Where legs and hands tangle and wrangle and press
Into their feeling places, making shivers
Out of the dark fiercer and fierier than slivers
Of clean sun by morning on shrill waters –

5
Nightwork, perforce alone to-night,
At sleepless 4 a.m., hating small hours radio,
And a scorner of unassisted self-abuse,
Has a very bright idea: rings Dial-a-Tit,
And listens to the wobbling.

6
What frankly feeble lover, even some hellfire
Sticker-up for Nature, does not go
Spare as Nightwork when the dawn chorus starts? That seeping,
Officious rant from the whole *Book of the World's Birds*
(With five hundred bloody colour plates.)

153

7

Night and its stations pass with clamped-up eyes.
What sleeping with adds up to is: an hour
Before you sleep, and later on, an hour
After you wake up, but before you rise
– Between the two, some eight hours spent so dead
You, like Old Nightwork, might as well be dead.

131 *Vincentio Hangs On*

if I went, thought arrogantly the Duke, someone else
        would have to be saved from it all by my coming back.
                This time he was not humble and did not go.

Christ! things were bad. Ignoring Government appeals,
        the plastic bottles blocked up the underpass. Build
                us a flyover, their spokesman demanded.

the people were urged to economise by Ministers.
        One said: Using the cores of toilet rolls
                as toilet rolls, would help us at this time.

the militants had halted the mushroom farms.
        Fungi were growing on the mushrooms.
                'Their wives say "Go back",' showed a poll.

the Duke, not having left, could not go back.
        He could not even come down like a god
                from a Supersonic-Channel-Tunnel-Machine.

the thermometers offer to the mercury: Accept a cut
        to Centigrade rates for now, and we will consider
                talks about Fahrenheit scales next year.

yes, television slashed to seven channels, only six coloured,
        closing down at twelve, the intelligentsia
                forgetting the words of the commercials.

students, disguised as guides, got into the grottoes, wiped
    the drips off the stalactites, caused tourist
        income to plummet, never caught the swine either.

exclaimed the Duke: The breathers are behind all this,
    breathing in, out, day, night, agitating to share
        the very air with us who – respire.

you must conserve rubber corkscrews, said an announcement,
    steel corkscrews are just as good, in twenty years
        all bottles will be made with corks again.

the four faces of a public clock showed each a different
    time. Thought the Duke: Some liberal, giving
        the workers four chances of being punctual.

photos of an agribusinessman fondling a battery hen
    were printed by conservationist subversives,
        and sparked off a community crisis.

to reap the full benefits of restriction, a newspaper wrote,
    we must face higher prices for things which will be

                                                    cheaper
    when less is more available than it is now.

after a hundred years or so of this, people were saying:
    Are we sure we need a Duke, whether he knows
        he is coming or going or not?

Waiting circa 1949, in the little waiting-room
Beside the single track, with the small stove crackling,
Reposed on a bench, reassured by a verified connection,
The journey onwards going twenty miles
To a destination feeling remote (no seagulls
Floating in this far from the unreachable marshes)

He listens to the quiet and contemplates distance:
The long miles slowly to go in the two carriages,
Then the light in the wrinkled panes of the door,
And the known face opening and greeting.

Three hours before he had been: a philosopher,
Recounting in a lecture *things we can be certain exist,*
The other side of the moon, for example, which cannot be
seen
But may reasonably be inferred. An hour and a quarter
To wait.
            A low fence exists, he sees it, on the far
Side of the track, and a dimmed field beyond, leaves lying
Dulled by the rain, circa 1949 and autumn.

The stove, for now, inextinguishably secure;
And hard corner-arms to repose on, in the straight seat
In the somewhere surely-coming small train;
Then all the villages ahead, reached singly,
The place with a market, the one with a harbour . . .
Trees brushing the windows, darkened grass along cuttings,
A known face of the moon veiled above the coppice.

And the little room was secure at the time,
And stayed so, carried in the mind when the station
Closed and the track was wrenched up, and the
Stove broken out of the wall.
Life, Elizabeth, he said, *is certain to get*
Imperceptibly faster and more brazen. And later, *You*

Were always some distance to reach, but
Today, how everything feels too close . . . is much too seen.
We die, these days, of the obvious and the near.
We die of the marshes towed to the caravans in
Half-an-hour.

        He is dying today, in a twelfth floor room
With a high steel crane veering outside the window, higher.

But delay, blessed delay, yet. Thinking time. An hour
And a quarter to the end.

              Dear Elizabeth. Just to say
I shall come by train in the usual way.
I shall have the wait at Charnham for contemplation.
I ought to be with you by just after five o'clock.
Don't trouble to meet me, I have little to carry. And

It is a mere ten minutes' walk from the station.

A Song of Good Life (133–153)

133 *Natural Order*

Over the dainty
Crenels of a dynasty,
The sweep of old, walled,
Outspread estates:
Pheasants fumbling through hedges,
Trotting peasantry.

In one high, green drawing room
A photographer is spreading a tableau out,
Standing, seated, sitting on the floor;
A dynastic tableau.

Try to look royal and natural
At the same time. Try to look
Ordinary. Is it so hard?

Sweeping in hushed cars,
Naturally,
To platforms of bunting,
Shaking dignitaries and their hands,
Stooping a solemn wreath to green again
The limbs and bones written into historical mud.

At births and weddings and deaths,
In dynastic succession,
Outspread sweet fanfares,
Gold Stick Extra-

ordinary,
In black, trotting carriages,
Dynasties of quadrupeds.
Can it be natural, please?

Today it has to be natural through the streets,
Learning to fix quite ordinary
Poses into the viewfinder,

Learning to green a nothing
With a mask of naturalness,
Ordinary smiles, no crenels,
An outspread dynasty of masks.

134 *The Telephone in his Office*

The answers are freshly delivered, complete,
Infallible, natural, good-humoured,
In the light of, thank you
To the press of cameras and questions at ten,
After rising, shaking, at six,
After a session of member countries till three.

Now flying to Washington Moscow Saigon
Cairo Jerusalem Brussels,
In power above the cloudbank in the light of
The sun, hands shaking with heads-of-state,
Or talking to them on the telephone
In his black office, in an ordinary morning.

Ceremonial luncheon for the Ambassador of,
And Madame. Avoiding the migraine lights
In the prisms of jewels. The working together
For the common good, in the light of
The historical bonds.

The index shaking through the afternoon,
The mind, if not the face or hands,
Shaking while conferring to curb the,
On measures to prevent the,
Review surcharges in the light of.

In the light of an ordinary afternoon like this,
He could go into his office,
Pick up the one, coloured, one-coloured telephone,
And in twenty minutes
Fifty million people would be dead.

135   The Majesty

Wishing to be thought of brisk but leisured at toilette, the decisive, scrupulous shaving, the braces bracing the Queen's Own shoulders for the day. Not this no-man's land between pulsing half-sleep and the muddy light of the forecourt.

And breakfasting at six off immaculate silver; lifting, on a sideboard, burnished salver-lids like domes from an imperial age, coffee attentively poured, and one bending who trots out again with an oiled flip and whisper of the door. But: fumbling from cupboard to table with slices from a polythene wrapper, time only to open at the obituaries . . .

Still, the scattered particulars of the outspread city, the bus queues in the rain, the underground, the people about their occasions, can all be swept together into the purview and protection of the Law, comprised in its ancient cohesion, chastened by its sanctions.

This evening, addressing a society: 'A High Court Judge Remembers': *We enshrine all our age-old, historical, meditated wisdom in the majesty of the Law, which holds, through all its manifold detail, our Christian society together. If the Law is brought into disrepute, if the Law is flouted . . .* And, colloquially: *Many other comic, and indeed tragic, sides of life come one's way in a day in Court.*

Home to the nightmare of the giggling crucifix.

Caption: *Simon Kemberton – things moving fast*
Among the Op-Art

Unruffled, King's Road-suited Simon Kem-
berton of Paramore
Is the type of the new, young executive with a bright
Eye to the European future. *Forescan* found him
In his Op-Art panelled office on
The nineteenth floor of the newest Seifert block
In the City Centre, eight multi-coloured
Telephones blossoming around him. The story
Of Kemberton's rise is amazingly simple,
Based on accurate, split-second
International contact with his fifty million
Market, getting producers to package the product
Brightly the way supermarkets can sell it
To the lady with the little wire tray. Business
Has grown just ridiculously fast since Paramore
Adroitly skirted round that take-over bid
From Dave Walker's Hubris empire.
The future, a bright one,
With branches in Brussels, Jerusalem,
Cairo, Saigon, Washington, you name it,
Looks to be a rather pleasant trip
To the multi-million level.
Forescan asked Kemberton how he, why he,
What he, etc., etc.

137   *Rustic Wedding*

The son of the plantation farm that takes
A company name
Is driving from the edge of the fen to his wedding
In one of the collapsing churches.

His bride in the mistery
Steps out of her Vanden Plas in a turquoise cloud
Of unnatural fibres for which a thousand hens
– In no particular order – have pecked in the dark.

Worming into the pews for New English maxims
Under high Norman vaults, their guests are there by treading
Down hedges and trees for miles, and renting
Wet cottages out to 'peasants' and the wind.

At the reception hotel,
A sweet lulling music blows, all the time,
Through every sort of room.
                           They'll sit and talk
The latest, lucrative, pollutants; over Veuve Clicquot.

138   *Interview with a Creator*

No, not the idea of slamming at people with the stone
From the start.

We begin with the product itself,
And make it into something which people can be persuaded
To want of their own free will.
What we do is, we adapt
The image of the stone.

Take this picture of the stone in the Supplement,
The grain of its firm arm around the brunette
On the undulating fields of County Down.

– Or, if you like,
We soften the stone.

Between the News and the Quiz the
Giggling little rubber stone frisks
And carols around the screen
With a backing of sweet music from a combo
Of pliant pebbles.
A voice confesses:
I never bought any other stone since I first tried this.

Walking the outspread supermarket glades, Mrs Bourn
Sees the price reduced on the turquoise packaging
Round the offer of succulent stones. And some stones
Nestle in her tray at the check-out instead of bread.

Two minutes only in lightly-salted water,
And they slip down the smiling throats at the table
With no trouble at all.

Mrs Bourn's young family of seven can't wait
For their dainty stones.

139   *Arranged Blossoms*

Peeling itself away like a morsel of skin,
There's another petal to be seen to,
Deranging the antique order of the room.

She must get Mr Fernlock to cast her again.
Knowing the right things to do, the investments,
The Settlement, the family, is so hard.

Angela can be so very hard.
One can't give straight advice as one can face-to-face
When the two of them are in Johannesburg.

Well, I can't stand the weather here either.
But this is my home; and Angela,
You might try writing more often than you do.

Dust the Wedgwood now, not later, it's waited two days.
She must get herself cast again, horoscopes
Can alter for the better, she has heard this.

Tuesday already, and so much to do before Friday.
Friday is the car to Mr Goodman's
To get the codicil witnessed.

And things going wrong she can't manage herself,
Yes, that tap thumping ever since last Thursday week.
A dirty man, who smoked, and it still won't stop.

140   *Warmth*

What made her decide she'd
enjoy being a wee-hours disc-jockey,
well it was something about *giving*
to ordinary people, and well . . . And
did she like the life now (and how!)
she was part of it, yes she thought
it was a great life, what did she
especially like about it, providing the
sweet music between the News
bulletins, what made it a good life
for *her?* Well, maybe, like she said,
she felt she was doing something
for people. But switching this
round, what was it people did for
her? Well, people were quite
wonderful to her, she couldn't

164

describe it, it was a kind-of warmth,
you know, coming over to you from
people. As to being the most
popular girl in England to phone in
to, she could only say, giggling
shyly, she loved talking to people,
and though you did get those who,
well, just couldn't get *over* to you,
well, most of the time, you know, the
kind-of warmth, she thought it was just
great. Would she sum it all up, then,
in the same kind-of thing, the kind-of
warmth she felt? Yes, she couldn't
describe it exactly, but it was maybe
just that thing, a kind of . . . warmth
she got from nothing else.

141 *In the Trade*

Pre-empted places in the breakfast car,
Death commuted to the Midlands by
The mercy of trade.

Having to really know the ways
Of the production line, the likely
Delivery dates and everything,
That's the point.
And smile and be at ease, make the customer think
He has thought of it for himself.

Eight-ten.
The older man instructing the younger
With age-old wisdoms nodded quickly and taken in,
As curios, as bygones. Off-the-hook talking
To King's Road hung-on-you, wily eyes
Watching the trade for years,
Wily eyes for slugs on the lawn at home.

We shall have to work even harder, and watch
The Japs, we really will. It's not the old
Shoddy stuff now, you know, oh no.

The Midlands are coming, Birmingham coming nearer
Past grey sheep chewing
At scrubland fields. *That's England for you,*
This table-cloth should be absolutely white.

And *I left him the literature, you never know.*
Now you and I, being in the trade, we know . . .

The firm is, for the moment, in the trade.

142   *Going Up*

After a year or two among the drop-outs,
One motivated drop-out
Dropped out, & took his paperback Tolkiens & his
Guitar to another part of town.

It was high summer, the workers were striking, & he was young;
& he bought himself a girl by computer, because
He had dropped out after getting a 2/1 in Maths
(& that after smoking a lot the night before).

& to borrow the money he went to a father
Who clutched at straws, & he set up in business
With a shop full of bygones and modest antiques
In a district where a famous estate agent used

Meat-porters, working spare-time, to get Vacant Possession.
But to be fair, he did not cut his hair
(Which Jani trimmed) and he did not chuck his jeans,
And he even smoked a little now and then.
                                                              Well,

Soon the fully-converted, waste-disposing, Georgian
Terraces filled with young sales executives,
Barristers, painters, young dons with a line on linguistics,
And their shop was full; and this pair sold Vic-

torian jam jars, Valentines, oil-stoves, tea-urns,
Shelves of pith helmets, sugar-tins, chamber-pots,
Phonograph cylinders, pincushions, ballads
With flaked yellow covers; and old solitaire boards

On which dainty marbles, quick and bright,
Ran round the bevelled edges, round and round
Going 'Clink! Clink!' They bought a villa in Minorca,
And they called their children Siddhartha, Demian and Tim.

143 *The Card*

A young dark suit
A tie with crests
A death's head sheared bright
From a two-pin plug
Over coffee at eight
Yes by all means phone
I'll be in my office
Would you like my card
That's the number here
I've written my number at home
Any time except Sundays
(The roadhouse Sundays
Lunch at the Motor Hotel
A bar with leather sofas)
Take as long as you like
You'll forgive me a moment –?
Well you might like to think of
You'd be well advised to consider
No we don't give a discount

Don't hurry about a decision
The other possibility of course
In the light of the surcharge
Not the same depreciation
I have one of them myself
Yes perhaps think it over
Yes call in to-morrow by all means
We stay open till six
Lightly walking in every
Morning over the forecourt
Supple death's head
In the plate-glass
Biro and Handy Guide
On an alcove desk yes
By all means by all means by all means by all means

144   *She Made of It*

Cords hitched up, sweater pulled down
Over a plain human body absorbing itself with semantics
Among the dried leaves.

Walking along this path, this October,
Having committees to talk with Bill Stennett, and
Uncategorised air to now and again
Replace hair from in the wind.

At the wheel of the Renault, later,
Towards her flat with the two upstairs levels,
Two steps down from one to coffee on the other,
Thinking, if pressed to say,
Of bubbles in a steel tube neatly rising.

Faint photostats from *Mind*, uncurled and
Flattened from the copier, clammy, smooth
And grey, at angles to the bevelled
Table-edge. – Straighten them, in passing.

Eight years ago those two nights
In a borrowed room when some people who, at the time,
Were in Colorado, left them the key to use.

Not since. And she never made
Notes for the bother of nostalgia (for example:
The cactus paling stiffly on the ledge,
And the klaxons blaring meanwhile for sins downtown.

And she wouldn't recall the place-mats of *Berkshire Scenes*.)

145 *An Evening with Anne*

Don't stop what you were saying, I'll see to another record;

Where was I? Oh yes, at *that* I sat up and opened my ears and put
two and two . . . He'll evidently be moving to that Division in the
New Year;

Where he'll have to try to learn to live with Benther, agreed,
which I wouldn't care to have to do myself. But for him it'll be a
decided step up all the same;

Someone, perhaps I shouldn't say who, told me Pat (Ferguson)
would be going to the Regional Department in the Spring, working
on the nineteenth floor. You can guess how she arranged *that;*

Which means Peter Daines will be bound to get the Senior IV
post at Colswell (unless they appoint from outside, which they
hardly would). And he's only been in his present job one year;

Anyway, not to bore you, but they've asked me to move into
Jean Levitt's office, temporarily anyway. Yes, quite a surprise, and
I'm not so sure I can cope; but I said I would. I mean, it seemed a
chance, and it leaves me the option of getting out later, or moving up
higher when the time comes, if it does. It leaves me completely free.

Try again. No? Vivaldi actually.

146   *Vital*

I think my work is important, I am a link
In a long chain.
I had to have the training for it,
And I had to dirty my hands.
They ask my advice when they want to know what would be
                                                        best.
I might move up even higher, in time.

One Sunday I woke up shouting. She said,
What on earth's the matter, we're supposed to be
Going out to dinner later; or rather lunch.
I dressed, and played with Lynda, and
Felt a bit better.

I was called into the office from the shop
Floor. 'Mr Fletton, up from London, wants to see you.'
But I was hearing the mutter–mutter,
The kind-of giggling noises inside the machines
Through four thick concrete walls.
I could not read the words in front of my eyes.

She said last Thursday, you haven't said a thing
The whole evening.
I said no, I've been watching.
. . . I couldn't name a thing I'd seen on the screen.

Today is vital, people are relying on me
To get ten thousand packages out on time.
I am part of a chain, a link, they ask my advice.
I open the front door. After the wind,
It's a lovely cool morning, and sun;
Very bright.
The keys of the Toledo are clenched wet
In my right hand. And I don't move.
I am standing shaking. I am standing, shaking.

147 The Image

Vampires are said to be living in Essex this Sunday morning. And the paper he buys for serious reading says, in the Supplement, 'Most of us would resort to cannibalism if there was nothing else we could do.' As if it were a sign, the shaft of cool sunlight strikes down through the R.A.F. window onto the Communion rail and young Mrs Mountacute, with leukaemia, kneeling. The Christian and Property, The Christian and War: people like to have it all made clear. Or, shall we say, the context for their personal decisions made clear. He tidies the bookstand in the alcove, and shakes the box inquisitively; but wouldn't wish to be seen opening it just now. Down the gravel path past the graves, past the Dormobile (it won't depreciate as much) and into the rectory, and the cooker is pinging for lunch. Must ring and check with the group performing after Evensong.

148 Metres

Reads, alone, last thing at night:
Make life a rhythm,
A strenuous, glorious rhythm,
Live it, feel it, in every muscle and limb,
A beautiful, disciplined, natural
Rhythm.

And every part is ready for waking:
The shoulder that hinges
The arm that flexes
The wrist that sends
The finger that stops
The alarm at 5.45.

Pill from the phial in the cabinet,
And click the cabinet shut to fix
The mirror of a really healthy face.
– Washing to a rhythm, cleaning teeth, etc.

Slapping the streets of Wythenshawe with fit plimsolls,
The stadium-terraces, the crimson number
Jogging on the vest
On the drizzling Saturday screens.

Back, and eating sensibly, lightly,
The Corporation offices, 8.30 exactly
– And make life a rhythm
On through your working day;
Whatever your work, it can be done.

I hear the new appointment in the Data Section
Is a bit of an athlete by all accounts.

149 *An Actress*

The part for now: kimono and Bianco,
A finish to the long day at the agency.

I couldn't live in small rooms these days:
'Spacious, second floor, deep freeze provided,
Just off Gloucester Road.' Rather garish
And 'a slum really', I read somewhere . . .
But I like it.

And visited once in three months by a father satisfied with a
Capable girl, he shrugs and supposes.
Can look after herself.

A Range Rover using the Residents' Parking,
A French registration. *René!*
Hi, I'll let you in! An Entryphone
Can keep out anything that threatens to be
Embarrassing.

Réne, have a seat, dump the books on the floor.

Oh, you're harder at twenty-six, I feel that.
Christ, a hell of a night, you can say, and then
– All over!

Yes, if life is responding I do respond.
Yes, I'm sure I respond,
There are lots of things I respond to.
I think he called himself René. (An actress
Will make any noise she considers suitable.)

– But Amanda, Christ, what a giggle, did he
Talk in French when he came?

150 *Imposing*

In the middle of late September a commissionaire,
Outside, from the pavement in front of, the curtilage of,
The Majestic Hotel, kicks a scrawny
Leaf away, underpaid;
A leaf that must not be allowed to stay.

He can summon taxis in a chocolate brown, braided
Majestic hat, even when it is
Chucking it down for bus queues.
He can impose it, on even such a street.

What it is is to have grown into his hat,
His long long coat, his bright thick shoes,
To have grown into this from being a sergeant once
(Now, for the management, ordering a leaf about)
And the matching suit, and the accurate watch:
The time, for the residents.

You do not grow out of it if you are in this,
Ever. But leaves
Will somehow enter the front, revolving door.
And there will be, the week after next, a leaf
Scratching inwards somewhere on the second floor.

151 *Circle*

Chris's place . . . They'll have something . . . Last time a whole
week coming out of a bad one & not eating. Nothing but beautiful
books at first with blossoms on the outside, & he read them for years
& saw unending spread-out brown stone valleys of these thin
millions of bodies dipping their limbs in supple mud & flowing
slime . . .

then the words were suddenly changing into these smiling faces
or masks, altering as he looked from yellow & black to sparkling
green, above a cloudbank. & he tried to fix his mind on them as
words, but they wouldn't mean themselves, they were the faces. &
he tried to fix on the letters in the words but the letters were faces as
well, & through the circles of the O's like pulsing vaginas he was
trying to get out, but they clenched . . .

& out was a succession of streets & streets of food-shops, the
food in them, the meat, was bright packages of muddy bandages, or
shit, or little glittering clusters of hazy lights & blossoms & beautiful
books, everything changing colours & then going dead flat & going
dead flat . . .

he said, *Don't come to me with white coats & sympathy.*

152 *The Gloves*

Bent with close eyes in the late afternoon,
Concentrated alone at a nearby bare
Velveted window which spreads out
Exquisitely a random few pedestalled pairs
Of grey gloves carefully drooped.

An infinity of care gazing at
An easy deployment of care
– The gloves not visibly priced.

174

She would need to go in to enquire the price,
In a voice that would not fit
From a voice that has learnt to fit.

The long sour ache of being this much poor
Was earned through generations, and comes
To such aspirings of the menopause:
Treating herself with the gloves,
With the look of the gloves.

The dustless tableau of the window
Stays where it is, where it always has so far.
Better to go back, as she will,
With bare hands on the underground, on
The disappointed journey, her fingers keeping
Apples and a small loaf covered in the polythene.

153 *Twilight*

Outside the window,
Over the black brick wall,
The hearses were there again today,
Black hushed carriages
Passing and pausing, the stench in here increasing,
The shapes through the curtains I pulled across.

He was late again last night, so where had he been?
The hearses were bigger today,
Standing or sitting I could see them,
And the thump of the box I could hear
In the heart of the cold tap. And it's dusk now,
Like lids of boxes on us all.

I told you, stop that, stop screaming,
The seven of you.
He'd been round to her again, I could
Tell it by his eyes, they faced me out
As I stood at the table, and washed the things, and asked.

So I told him.
Yes, I was positive, the doctor said, and the doctor's nurse

said,

I imagine that's the answer you wanted?

No, he can't himself, and he won't recommend,
It's the Law. No one will
Recommend anything, no.
We shall die, I suppose, and be bones in their mud.

Because they won't stop the hearses every day,
They won't stop, the streets of them,
The streets and streets of them,
The streets and streets and streets of me.

★　★　★　★

Seven Old Men on an Inter-City Train:
A Yeatsian Poem

The First.   Is that a flood or a lake?

The Second.   I saw a lake.
              And were there flooding there would not be
                                                      swans.

The Third.   The swans could have come from a lake, with
                                                all this rain
              A lake could overflow and spawn a flood,
              And cast out swans on it.

The Second.   Yet I look again,
              And see they are not swans but clumps of
                                                      suds
              Engendered by detergent. Had you but looked
              You would have seen all their necks were
                                                under water.

The Fourth.   But it is unimaginable that suds
              Should drift in wandering pairs as if designed
              To have the look of swans. Now the train has
                                                      passed,
              I speak it with an old man's memory,
              Yet say that nearly all of them were in pairs.

The Second.   Why should not some base tycoon-man, who
                                                      desired
              The pride of an environmentalist,
              Discharge the effluent of his factory
              So that, upon a sudden dreaming glance,
              It looked like swans?

The Fifth.   That would enhance
              A desolate vulgar place, could it but have
              Appearances of companionable swans.

The Sixth.   The poet Yeats loved real swans on real lakes,
              And had a penchant for using them as symbols.

The Third.	And Yeats, I have heard tell, wrote of swans on floods.
The Second.	But what would Yeats have thought of clumps of suds Reclining ceremoniously on a foul scene? To forge his symbols would be difficult. Yeats was not of an age when factory waste Was put on show as swans as a P.R. stunt.
The Fourth.	But Yeats himself was a bit of an old . . . tycoon, And symbol swans are just as shadowy As foam that moves upon a twilight flood.

The Sixth.	Yet
	                                                            Yeats
	Would not have cried the praise of effluent-
	                                                            swans
	To sanctify some tycoon's greedy till.
	Yeats was—

The Seventh.	I think that Crewe is the next stop.

155   *Spring Elegiacs at the Sea*

High on a ladder just began
The checking of the fairy lights for spring;
And a hundred yards on, a man
Digs about in some concrete tubs, planting

A glossier little-flower-decor
Than the girls—out of uniform, all white-
Faced in the wind sweeping the door
They shelter in—provide, on this first bright

Day of the new season. Menus
(Re-photocopied, but with changed prices)
Inserted into glass frames, views
Of the beach all now in colour, ices

In virgin, unexcavated
Blocks in the freezers, early posters for,
One would say, uncelebrated
Entertainers all start to beg favour

Of visitors. It's not yet May,
However, so the lights, blue, white, red, green,
Blue, red, green, white, a neat array
Of regulated colours, have not been

Time-switched for the evenings; but come
Easter and the first arrivals they might be,
And all the girls, and even some
Of the boys here, will start vaguely

Wondering what the season could bring,
And trek the long promenade, up and down,
Hoping out new faces dropping
Into their transitory gleaming town,

Which vanishes inside itself
In winter, hiding such summer young.
And so I walk here round about 12th
April, when the last spring tide which flung

Grit all over the forecourt of
The Pier Hotel is a week behind;
And they stand here, boys in half-love
With the girls, and the girls in a thrilled kind

Of love for themselves and for what
A girl is, unknowingly confined to
Their ancient, sweet limits.
                              One, not
Twenty-five yards away just now withdrew

From her quivering assortment
Of growing-up friends, and ran to an old
Lady treading the strait pavement,
Calling 'Gran!' At which, forgetting the cold

Day she shuffles through, the old one
Turns now and smiles, and the two stand to chat
– Linking the young, in the white sun,
With the very old, in the old skin that

Clothes her, a shrivelled Olympian
Admiring the girl with an elder's wise smile,
A sudden warm in her face when
She sums up the pursuits of the child while

The holidays last, all the parts
Of her granddaughter's body trembling for
Their inheritance, all the arts
Her nature will learn for itself: the lore

Of being a sexed creature,
Though the girl would not think of it like this.
The girl seems happy, in feature
And gesture, as she talks; then, with a kiss

For her ancestor she goes back,
And the elder goes on, with that old pride
In children's children and their lack
Of foreknowledge.
                        But mostly she will hide

Her close, quiet thoughts about today,
Which are these (though not so worked-out, of course):
'My own body has gone its way
Through the ways of her, but come to no worse

'Or sadder place, in the event.
From where I am, out of the surge of things,
All her mild being looks intent
On questing after toys. Her small age brings

'Her nothing, no, that I would have
Back again, having seen the whole game through.
It was all a dance of warm, slave
Shadows that I remember. And, when new,

'It was too strange to be enjoyed,
And as it went on, it was just craved for
Out of a habit. Time destroyed,
But cleansed me, also, I am sure

'– All this you'll learn, my eager sweet,
By living thousands of bewildering hours,
Starting this moment, in this street,
Arranged in sunshine, playing at being flowers.'

156 *The Seventh Knight and the Green Cat:
A Variation on the Gawain Poet*

Curious about her seven daughters, in turn came
The seven fortitudinous knights. And the first
To sit by the swarming fire, sipping mead with
Mother and eldest daughter, saw with much delight
The white cat pace to him, as he loved them,
Cats.
       The creature was unbleached to a queer
Shifting shade of green by the colours of the room
– Green hangings, green velvet on the couches,
Green branches at the window, green eyes in matron and girl,
Green even in the flames of the fire because
They cast salt in the crevices of the coals to
Make matching colours.
            So the white cat
Mewed at him, nudged his ankle, mounted his lap,
And the mother murmured, 'You are honoured, she
Has never before walked in such a way up to a man.'

This flattery went deep, proposals were made, and the pair
Duly wed.
                            And since daughters must dutifully marry,
And mothers must needs be mothers, and marry off,
A second knight came seeking the second daughter
And chose a green chair by the great fire while
The mother poured wine.
                            And willingly again the white
Cat rose on her green cushion, stood stretching,
And pattered the flagstones to the handsome second knight
To form fond figures-of-eight round the man's thin legs.
'There's a something about you that attracts her, she
Has never lingered with a man,' the lady said;
And in this style was her second daughter secured
To a cat-adoring knight.
                            This way it went too
With the third, the fourth, the fifth and the sixth, on
A succession of green days with the cat casually
Trusting its truly-said-to-be-untypical
Affection to the different knights, whether of
Transylvania, Tartary, Aragon or Tibet, being
Similar only in their peculiar pride at pre-empting,
Uniquely, an unsociable animal unsure of men:
Cat-lovers, but gullible with it, which is rare.

On the last and greenest day, green curtains gathering
Across the storm which sent green branches seething
Over the sky in a frenzied trellis-work of green,
The seventh knight finally knocked; one who knew
And loved cats more than any of these lovers, and
He yearned for the youngest daughter's hand.
                                          Her mother
Decanted liquor as usual, and the lovely daughter sat,
And green flames flashed in the hearth as the cat
Began again, greenly, its meaningful trek of the floor.
'She will not go to you, she has never yet greeted a man,'
The matron predicted; but the cat pounced all at once,
From no definable angle, onto the very codpiece of the doting
Knight, and neatly nestled.

                    So the mother and girl
Cried equally with eagerness and ecstasy as before

– At which this knight bounded up from his bench of green,
Shouting, 'I am getting out of here at once!'
And 'I know what sort of a situation this is,'
Dropping the cat, flat-eared and snarling with dire dismay,
And decapitating the thing with a dirk;
With screams from all, except himself and the evil cat's
Head, which jeered, and rejoined itself to the body
And said, 'What was that intended to imply?'
'The true friend of cats,' said the knight, 'knows
That cat in ninety-nine which walks for women
And not for itself alone, the animal which is
The familiar of witches.
                    But it seems as if
I did not exorcise this one quite enough.'
'You are remarkably right,' said the reconstituted cat
Sapiently, 'and for this wisdom you will wend,
By a promise you will here and now provide,
One year through numerous travails of the world, and come
To the terrible temple of the cat-goddess,
Mere pictures of whom inflict fevers and death on
Temerarious beholders who brave them, and
Leading lady of many a savage psychotropic
Trance. There we shall truly meet again,
And I shall take my turn.'

                    So the seventh knight
Ground on grimly over the bogs and crags of the world,
Lodging roughly, going rudely his slow way
On a bewildered horse through innumerable bleak,
Colourless, sleazy, subtopiate regions,
Demoralizing tracts of megalosuburbia,
And came, just after eleven heavy months, to a splendid
Castle, where his welcome was very grand.

And there,
In the course of prattle at dinner about property prices,
He thought he might try to elicit where the temple
Of the great cat-goddess stood, half-hoping it had not
Survived redevelopment.
'My fine fellow, I can
Tell you the lie of the land,' said the lord his host,
'But linger a little while here, enjoy some relaxation'
– And his lady smiled in sly sympathy and accord –
'While I do some terribly tiresome hunting. And, by the way,
Be good!'
With a feeling of distant *déjà vu*,
The seventh knight agreed; and for three successive days,
Was allowed to lie lazily in his bed while his host
Went hunting and left his lady (just as he had read);
Because, in short, truncating a tangled tale,
Coming in sleek, scarlet, delightful garments,
She insisted on sleeping with him thoroughly each of the three
Days her husband was happily hunting the evening meal,
Which the knight agreed to with an anxious sense of
Compromise; and suspicion.
Each night, the master,
Hot and bothered and scenting himself, brought back
The special spoils of a strenuous day in the field;
For this supper asking nothing in return and reward
But the knight's good company in anecdote and carousing;
And on the last day, as promised, he provided
Instructions for reaching the great cat-goddess's place.

It proved a daunting plod over muddy areas,
An extremely unclean excursion, so that when the knight
Arrived there, both he and his horse exhausted,
Spattered in the saddle from travel, he thought it was his
tiredness
That stopped him from seeing where it was. But suddenly,
He saw it: a low, brick thing nearly hidden in the grasses
Of a thistly field, with peculiar peep-holes from which
Any occupant, sitting safely in a nook, could
Scan out.

Dismounting, the knight called, clearly, and as
Loudly as he was able, on whoever lurked inside to
Emerge; and there expeditiously appeared a
Truly tremendous cat, the size of a full-grown woman.
'As I promised and pledged I would do, in all duty,'
Stated the knight, 'I have travelled to the temple
Of the great cat-goddess, to pay the penalty for
Following up certain suspicions too rashly,
And acting in anger.'
     Then the cat mysteriously smiled,
Saying, 'Listen. As an artful knight, you showed
Some shrewdness in discerning a witch's cat;
As a truly brave one you moved boldly
Against a defenceless, domestic beast; as
A plodder you showed profound persistence
In going your way through the world for a year
To find out this frightful place; as a seizer of chances,
You lay three times with the lady of the castle,
Obviously not having offered any oath you would thereby
Break; thus an immaculate code of knightly
Tactics you have most tightly kept, and
Will be rightly rewarded.'
     At which the vast animal
Cast off its outer cat-costume and calmly stepped forth
As the seventh daughter, dressed in the delightful,
Scarlet, sleek garments of the mistress of the castle.

'I was,' she said, 'all the time secretly concealed
In the little anatomy of the cat, in the body
Of the lady of the castle you came to know a bit,
And the knight of the castle, my loving master and lord,
Was all the time my own dear mother in drag.
So on the basis of all that, you may bow and beg now
The hand of the youngest daughter you came to collect.
There is no way out.'
     So, haltingly heeding
These dreadful words, the dumbstruck fellow put
His proposals, too perplexed to do other, and the pair
Were rapidly wed.

                    And they went on to work through
Many years of irrefrangible, retributive wedlock
(For the daughter turned out termagant as well as witch);
But concerning these travails I cannot truthfully say
I am sad or sorry, and cannot make this knight seem
An object of proper pity: as a grown-up, I regard
Knights and knighthood and the mores and weapons
Of a warrior society as both juvenile and degrading.

157 *Ceremony*

The Old Fox glimpses the little bag passing
Furtively round. They are secretly
Collecting for him in the office, he is going to retire.

The little bag, something tells him, will be light;
Not with an excess of paper money either.
The Old Fox is not popular where he works.
The typists have given 2p, the Under Manager
Ten, the Manager puts in a fifty
And takes out thirty-eight.
. . . It might not reach two pounds.

For forty-three years' service, two pounds or less!
The Old Fox cogitates quietly at his desk
(So quietly not even his secretary divines
He is cogitating at all).
Well, he could act the martyr, he could break down and weep
In front of the whole staff at his presentation.
He could make an acerbic speech and scathe the lot.

He could, out of humility, refuse
To have them make such a fuss of him: 'Forty-three
Years in so happy a firm seems not so long.'
But he has another idea.

The Old Fox knows where they keep
The key of the cupboard where the little bag
Is hidden in a teapot at night.

The evening before,
On a pretence of tidying up loose ends,
He stays altruistically late, the last to leave,
He fetches the key, he opens the cupboard,
He takes out the bag,
And he puts in the sixteen five pound notes he has drawn in
                                        the lunch hour
Through the youngest clerk in the bank.

At his presentation next day, the Old Fox
Breaks down and gratefully weeps in front of the whole staff.

158 *Point of Honour*

On a wet South Coast night when even
Believers in rain and luxuriance are resenting
How drenched the leaves are on the trees outside
Their pelted windows, a dark-haired girl lies lamenting
How far love seems from any dreamed-of heaven
– As this egotist who has just straddled her, and cried,

And slumped into a heavy shagged-out quiet,
Says, reaching for a well-placed cigarette,
'If I'm hurting your right leg, dear, please let me know.'
And oh, it is her *left* leg which he needs to get
Clear of to reach the matches; having come to lie at
A clumsy angle during his last, slow,

Gratifying turmoil, which has nonetheless
Been too fast for the girl by half.
                              Now she has heard
Sam. Johnson's words, 'To scratch where there is an itch
Is life's greatest pleasure.' And she forgives her absurd
Seducer's selfish haste. And she feels worse distress
That he thinks it her *right* leg on his right side of the bed

– Since a gentleman could tell which limb was which.

I

Look down into hotels where girls work
            In their vacations,
And in the early evening, managers, averaging
Forty-six years old, induce them to upper bedrooms,
Empty because business is dropping off:
Think of the protestations round the coasts of England,
The moaning on the candlewick coverlets,
And the girls so young, this the first time for most of

                                                    them,
And the managers cautious and honourable,
Saying they won't go too far, and going
Too far, the girls done with A levels,
And the managers pressing and leering and the minds blown
                                                    for days.

II

Look down at one manager at seven-thirty, all his girls
            Heltering through his mind,
And fewer girls each year in the last three years,
But this year more girls than for three years past,
Five girls to be exact, so it is spring once more
And the blood sparkles, at an average age
Of forty-six. There he is now, leering in the glass
Behind the lounge bar, tilting, adroitly, Chartreuse,
Thinking of his five girls this season: Tina, Prue,
And Elaine, and Kirsten, who pulled the scarlet
Curtains herself, and Rosemary, queen of impermeable
Silence, who will come back of her own accord.

III

Look down there at the window of a room at dusk
    Where a pensive manager,
Letting the twilight change to dark, sits alone
Without a light at nine-thirty, run out of cigarettes,
Sits alone, eyes open, in a crumbling swivel chair.
Now he hears the feeble whine of a slow lift,
And a girl comes in who understands his sadness,
Business declining and years declining
– And a good love quickens in this very young girl,
Or a love upgraded from pity (she has brought some cigarettes)
    For a manager pining heavily in a hotel
Not doing particularly well . . .

IV

Look down at a boy friend emptying fruit machines
    On the pier at ten-fifteen,
After a fair day's business. The ogling machines
Are adjusted finely to concede just a little
And grasp the rest to themselves,
And this girl is adjusted finely in the same way
– Because of a manager of a hotel (where they
Spend the early evenings in an upper bedroom).
She is meeting the boy in the Bull, and
For him life feels like a nasty row
Of mocking variables, apples, plums and flags,
As he filches the coins with which he will buy the drinks.

V

And look at this boy friend at midnight
       At the girl's gate:
Now cradling the sobbing girl, who has told him
Everything all at once in a sudden gush.
She says she could be sick, which she could not,
And the boy is sick instead because it has taken
Eleven pale ales to her four bacardis-and-coke
To bring her to this point of revelation.
Thus: the manager, his girl friend, and her boy friend –
It's a bad time for all of them (though at this moment a
                                            letter
Is on its way to the girl to say she has
Two D's and an E and a place at the North-East Polytechnic).

VI

But look again at this boy friend, who is feeling better
       Up the hill past the Cats' Home
On his long walk back about an hour later.
He is compassionating the manager in question,
Whose letters he has been shown: 'Dear Tina,
I long for you all the time . . .' and similar things.
He can guess the timeless agony of the man,
Longing so much for the girl he more or less
Longs for himself, and he is not so jealous.
He could be in the same position one day.
He could be in the same . . . He is overcome
With a selfless presagement of the nastiness of time.

VII

    Look between the chink in the curtains
          In one hotel window,
Where a manager, at one-thirty, is turning a coverlet
Down, the only coverlet he ever turns
Down, to slink into bed beside his wife.
Groping the pillow in the darkness, this manager
Thinks of that day's baffling girl: 'You've never
Read any Gary Snyder or Frantz Fanon, you've hardly
Heard of Claes Oldenburg or Roland Barthes,
Or of Simon or Garfunkel,' she had said in reproach.
'Do you call that living?' – 'Yes,' he thinks,
As he thinks of her left breast flipping the back of his knee.

VIII

    In the terrible small hours look over
          Everyone fitfully asleep,
And do not imagine they do not have complex dreams.
E.g., a girl is at the bottom of a slimy pit
With smooth sides, and hairy managers are toppling
Hairy managers in rockers' goggles down on her,
So that she screams; only the scream
Comes out a bit ecstatically and she can't
Explain to herself why this should be really so,
Or how she should have come to be here at all.
It stays with her while she dresses for another
Long day at the hotel. She can't wait for the early evening to
                                  come round.

IX

Look into a corridor where a girl at nine-twenty a.m.
      Walks carrying sheets,
And a second follows, to shake them out with her,
One girl moderately appealing and the other
Less appealing than her, not least in her perceptions
(Which she keeps to herself). The conversation
Is equivocal, since they are discussing the manager
And the first girl has more to disclose than she says,
Though she is hinting, continually hinting,
In the faint breeze from the sheets. Small tabs with
Laundry numbers fall off the outflung linen,
And the bedroom radio sings of *'leurs déguisements*
                                   fantasques'.

X

Lastly, gaze out there at the crematorium.
      Having consumed fourteen
Tequilas in half-an-hour, a manager
Is being consumed to rest. His wife comes first,
And behind her follow forty-six girls in all,
The youngest sixteen, the oldest thirty-four,
And all in states of nostalgia or raw distress
According to how lately they knew the man.
So wife and girls compassionate each other
As the clergyman, noting an ancient English
Ritual of mourning, shakes each girl by the hand.
If this can happen, the world must be good. It is ten forty-five.

Lastly my turn to hide, so
The other children instantly
Scattered among the scrubland grass,
Blanked their eyes, began
To count aloud.
                             Away downhill,
The traffic thundered less
In the hazed streets, the orange
Street-lamps suddenly lit in
A necklace of twilight mauves. I was
Expected home from this game, to eat,
And read myself to sleep. Besides,
There were so many ruses more
I wanted to devise.
                             Before
They counted out my time, came
Running to look for me, I ran
And left them there, I ran back home
And left them.
                             Turning today
A tower-block corner, I saw them
In the gathering dark, bemused
And middle-aged, in tattered
Relics of children's clothes, still
Searching even now in the glittering
Scrubland of my Precinct, for
What had deserted them, what had
Cast them there; blank-eyed, and
Never to tell what I had built,
What I had left them with in forty years.

I laughed about it afterwards,
But it frightened me at the time.

Yes;
And in entertainment, one axiom is
That scare can be terribly funny:
Those floors that tilt you
Ludicrously here, there, here
In the House of Ghosts;
The wicked fangs on the posters
Dripping hilarious red.

The real worst of horror is
Its shabbiness . . . How nice
If all private scare were awfully
Amusing to retell,
And much better still
If it really, rather wickedly,
Entertained.

— I could hoist my habitual
Skull at its fixed
Mirror in the morning, go at it
Over its shallow covering with
The razor, and receive
Such a comical thrill.

I could open its mouth, gape
Wide with it, make a sound,
And laugh about it afterwards.
It could be a real scream.

When the Library of Congress is finally
Reducible to a cube one inch by one
Inch by one inch, you are going to need to lose
Absolutely nothing: stored and retrievable

A pear-core once left gangling on an ashtray,
The moment of Amanda's purple scarves touched
Sadly into order, the whole of *Le Figaro*,
And the accurate timbre of all your departed
Cryings-in-the-night. None of this
Will be vanishing any more.

Up there, instead of shining empty sky
(The still clear sunlight you are walking in
With terrors in your head) will be
A building specially built to set this right:

In any of a thousand rooms it will
Be possible for somebody to remain
For all of life after infancy till death,
Fed and evacuated and re-clothed
In a see-through cubicle, flicking up fact after
Fact and image upon image, actually
Playing his infancy back; working with his keepers
At the reasons, there, for needing to do such a thing.

163   *Afternoon in the Fens*

Then the farms ended, and the last dyke
Gave onto reeds, to mudlands; beyond which
A lightship blinked in the haze where the mud became the

                                             sea,

And that afternoon, two black and circling specks
Droned like gnats in that distance beyond our reach.

A dubious peace, the water shrunk down in the channels
Under clumps of bleached, unstirring grass;
A drugged end to August, the dyke-track
Dusty under four people's shoes where we stopped,
Gazing at a high square of wood braced

On a frame of iron in one field-corner. – And suddenly,
Out of the faint waters, the two droning dots
Enlarged towards us, two furies homing at this
Target we were standing near on the dyke, coming
Each ninety seconds and screaming and screaming

At the square of orange-painted slats clamped
On black poles of iron rusting into the rich earth,
Laying down fume trails onto smoke from the
Straw-fires left by farmers affluent on
Their steady reclamations of mud.

After two screamings our hands held our ears
As we moved aside along the narrow path,
But the two planes turning again over the flats
Avoided the target, were diving at, screaming at
Us, furrowing the air with billowing smoke-lines,

Homing at the four of us walking this bank
Between farms and land-finish. Out on the far sea
The lightship blinked to no one in the shallows,
And no one elsewhere moved in the fields
Under a sky impenetrably clear, curiously

Dulled by the heat-mists. Again and again,
Turning and screaming ancient, reasonless
Hatreds, they followed; then finally wheeled away, back,
Out over the sea, where the lightship continued to warn
Among sandbanks stuck with wrecks from recalled wars.

Sixteen miles from anywhere larger
On the map of a renamed county,
With an ancient market-square to which
Sore-faced farmers drive flocks in brown, tiered
Lorries every Thursday, is this
Country-town: a pestle-and-mortar
Restaurant, a glinting pharmacy
With rows of touched-up tincture jars, a
Salon of 'Gowns', one minimarket
Grocery, and a furniture shop.

Past the last black-and-white traffic sign,
The last lights in small manor-houses
Go out, and one more squirearchical
Day is done with; county magazines
Lie smoothly on their own in the dark,
The warm engines of the GL-12s
Click and settle in their garages
In villages where old bachelor
Campanologists tire, and hunger
At last, leave their ropes and sprint off home.

Through the glass of the furniture shop
A sleek room gleams, indescribably
Tidy and perfect: purple wall lights
Allure and chill, and a magenta
Carpet sets a table and two chairs
Fast in the specific attention
Of two poised lamps. This is a ghosts' room:
Two especially, two spectrally
Immaculate-feeling people could
Stop and repose here at two a.m.

As exactly pure exemplars of
How things ought to be. It would give them
That virgin bed with a canopy
In the background, spaced silken pillows
Asking those who have walked at a fixed
Distance for so long to lie, chastely
Apart, until the first unpolluted bird
Announces dawn. Shall we step inside?
I can't think we or it will ever
Suit each other quite so well again.

165   *The World Outside*

When poetry was a landscape art, arranging
Syllables in a noble sweep to gaze up, the vista
Was the big house of order and seclusion, stately
Between stiffly regular lines of most proper trees.
The world kept out was the goatherds and their pipes.

When *civitas* seemed quite possible, the view
Was the city square, across a purified *parole*
– Incredibly kempt, and engraved with some token bourgeois
Respectably strolling out. Small in the foreground, the rest of
                                          the world
Was the mongrel dog that whined at the flawless space.

Seeing the lift 'Out of Order' he mounts the stairs
Helped up by a loosening banister, and sees
Poetry striving to root in a tub of dying plants
Put down on a vinyl landing. The poor pale thing
Is hungry for sense and sanity, wincing at

The sight from this fifth floor window, and craving
Simply to understand: four lanes of a freeway
Mesh with six lanes of another below him, and the sun
Amazedly glitters off the flank of twenty-two
Office-floors across the street. At the ninth landing,

He knows that this world won't be excluded. It goes with him
Into a room where fifty are gathered together,
All drinking to efface the scenery. Traffic management,
Retrieval systems, God, can't contain this world;
So words will somehow have to.

                              'Hullo,' he says,

'I've read your book, I think it's really great.'

166　*Breach*

Within a mile of a sea, which could be heard,
On a Chesterfield much too narrow,
On a night that was much too short,
These two achieved a rare sort of victory:

They carried through a completely unselfish,
Unkind-to-no-other-people act of love,
Between twelve twenty-seven and twelve
Forty-four, while the latest oil slick

Slurped at the sands in the dark.
Nightlong coastguards fought it with radioed
Data about its location, helicopters clattered
To neutralise the thing with chemical sprays,

And half the resort was out next morning, waiting
As for some dismal, predicted second coming.
But these two made their protest about
The general soilure of the world at the hands

Of the effortful and the crude by just one
Once-only, uncontrived breach
Of its chaos with love. And there should be
A plaque on the esplanade to this effect.

167 Lost and Found

The knights on his first chess set were mounted
On horses with close-together eyes and narrow noses:
An amused look whichever way they faced.
One day, the set was not complete. A knight
Was lost, he played half-heartedly for thirty years
With a plastic pepperpot instead. She walked into his room
Eventually at forty-one, with a set smile
And amused eyes close together under her forehead.
She took a step, and turned aside, smiling.
Consequently life could be played properly again.

168 Procedural

The Old Fox sits at the front in the Chairman's eye, he
Questions the Apologies for Absence, he
Questions the Minutes, including
The accuracy of the amendments in these Minutes
To the Minutes of the meeting before last, he
Raises Matters Arising for half an hour.

Then he
Carps at the order of items on the Agenda,
Queries the omission of items *from* the Agenda,
Interrupts, interjects, raises Points of Information,
Asks innocent (loaded) questions, has serious Points of Order,
Puts down motions, puts down amendments to motions,
Puts down amendments to amendments, questions the voting,
Wants the Chairman to state again exactly what it is
They have decided by the voting,
Wants his disagreement with the Chairman's decision minuted,
Quotes the Constitution,
Waves the Companies Act.

The Old Fox proposes the creation of
Sub-committees, steering committees, working parties and
Working groups, and declines election
To any of them himself. Any Other Business
Is devoted to matters raised by the Old Fox alone.

When the time to decide the Date of Next Meeting arrives, he
Objects on sound grounds to every possible date.
The desk diaries wearily rise from dispatch cases once again,
The overcoats stay unbuttoned, the great white pages
Turn and flutter and the flutter becomes a wind
And the wind becomes a gale tearing
At the darkness outside the window,
At the darkness in everybody's soul in the steamed-up room.

When the storm subsides, the Old Fox
Has disappeared until the next time.

169   *Representational*

His mother's wrinkled gloves have been warm enough
For the glass of the table where they lie to steam a bit:
These three are sat on gold-painted cane armchairs
In the middle of a spa, the man quite readily benign,
And smiling at the seven-year-old boy, though he hasn't
Much to say, and he sucks a thin cigar.
                                        A lady
In a purple topcoat leaves the counter and brings,
On a green tray, coffees and orangeade, she glides
Into their circle deftly with a quiet, adaptable
Smiling. This December is cold, but the sweet
Orangeade shrills heavenly up the waxy straw, a cool
Perfect runnel over his tongue, it's 1974.

                                        His mother
Is flushed and laughing with the man, there they are
In the great wall-mirror on the far side of the room,
Laughing and flushed the two of them, the freer selves
They could always be if this were only art
– Oh, if this were only art, or even fiction! But still,
Small rewards and mercies hold good . . .
                                   And the little boy
Now draining the last sacramental droplets from the glass
Quite likes the man, and the sun is coming out.
The lady with her emptied tray makes an adult smile
For the adults, and a children's smile for the child;
Her petition forms on the counter, to which she returns,
Are nearly filled, so the Ring Road is nearly prevented.
                                        The man
Will have paid off the Datsun in just under five months' time.

170 *Dea ex machina*

The woman with legs long for her family,
And the man with short legs, a short-legged man,
Match perfectly in the kitchen before Anna comes:
Anna, after a decade, at the wrong moment, back.

The crockery is streaked, and rattled dry,
And will have to be re-washed better by hand.
'Start over!' Anna will say, being American,
And they will have to unmatch their thighs, which
Will be aching, and may be slightly shaking,
And wipe at least forks to make a snack for Anna, back
Oh God, on the scene after ten years gone and not regretted.

It took no little time for these two to match,
For each to find the words, and their legs to lodge
One against the other and the other one
Against the other one, respectively,
In a sort-of logical comfort.

So may not
The telephone, vicious in voice or in silence,
Or the neighbour, preening her jubilee rosette,
Or finally Anna returning, any second now
– An emanation from her own dishwasher, all
Streaked with happy tears – break
This decent duo up.

171 *Night and Sunrise*

The cog-wheel abrasions are at it again
On this first glinting day of March,
Swerving over any pale surface, fastening
Blips of a crazed illumination on
The walls, the carpet, the half-typed page.

So again the old half-humorous yearning starts,
For the life of the darkest months:
The sunless heavens, the velvet hours
When action soothes, and shadow into shadow
Glides for a shadow-satisfaction.

– And truly, the heart of the educationist
Rises in autumn, as dead leaves drift
Round blocks of switched-on light in heated rooms;
The colours of that season moderate
The strident freshness on those shoots of green . . .

Reproached one late June day, when she maintained,
'Dark nights, cold weather, cold women,
Those are what you seem to want!' I tried to say,
'Exegesis is so difficult in summer,
My eyes can't tell the words from the spaces

In a book read out of doors. Besides,
Your sunshine only lights the surfaces,
And deep down things the dearest darkness lives,
Where profundity waits to be dug for'
– When she put the book aside, and we went indoors

Discussing my eyesight and my character,
Regretful or happy that the nights were already
Drawing in, and she closed the curtains.
                                        Who had won
I could not tell. We let things rest between
The dark and light . . . But I was glad she stayed

To try the night, and see the dawn up for me.

172   *On the Day*

He thanks whoever-she-is for her thoughtful
Beneficence to him, in that visitation
In the early hours of the morning on the day
He travels up to hear what the X-ray meant:
Appearing out of a carmine snowdrift and
Lustrously uncovering; then extending
Such long quick legs around him, and pushing
Him widely awake to smile at the dawn for once.

If he remembers ruefully that no one now
Visits of their own free will, that you visit
All your dreams on yourself, still, either way,
His world comes right for a while. In the lift,
As it drops to the snowing street, he knows
That either some she, or some part of himself,
Wants to will him even yet into life again
– Something is pushing schemes for winning time.

It may rain on the crags, but down in the resort
Only a sunset breeze billows and fans the grey
Nap of the boating lake into pink ripples, like
– Like scarlet ripples. Now, swiftly, she closes up
Her curtains on their small and disappearing day,
And turns with a wan smile. He sits with one hand warm
From her electric fire, and keeps the other cool
On the smooth rexine flank of her armchair. They dress
Formally, for tonight. And on the sideboard next
The window, on her right, stands a neat cut-glass pair
Of sweet aperitifs. He will not look her way,
But focuses the ashtray on its leather strap,
Where she may lately have set down her cigarette:
Nothing has yet deranged its drawn-up thread of smoke.
Whatever they may do when dusk has turned to dark
Is hidden from us yet (was hidden from us then)
So all we might conjecture from their perfect poise
Is that the most she feels concerning his profound
Conviction of her cold, impermeable grace
Is a sympathetic spiritual regard;
And envying their world of carefully-defined
Limits and chances (they need never travel on
To places where correct patterns of gesture make
No real impression on the bloody flux of things),
I can see reasons why, some forty years ago,
The self I am today should 'Spend a Day in Hove'.

174 Find

The waxwork chef once gripped in two wax hands,
Grinning over it at his readers, a menu
In a square wooden frame. The frame is empty,
And the chef lies grinning on his side in an overlooked yard
Behind a washeteria; presenting his lack of choice
To the gush of a drainpipe.
                              When they learn
The value of this site, and finally all
The bulldozed earth clumps down on him, he will make
A find for a commercial archaeologist: he will mean
Someone's failure to make it in this world.
He did not work. He does not work tonight,
In the little darkening yard.
                              So call it flesh
To ashes, and wax to wax: in the crumbling
Sewers of the city the waters are rising, the eating
Is going on in another, lighted place.
On this raining night, successful faces elsewhere
Shine out like artifacts of burnished wax.
                              They read,
Through their private spectacle-frames, what wine
Might gush from the list held out by the living hands.

175 Syllabics

At a deep pool left by a high tide high on a beach,
Rather sinisterly dark green even near its edge,
And rapidly shelving away to an unknown depth,
A various, bustling, organised family
Plays happily on through an overdue summer day
At the forming of little well-fashioned knolls of sand
With the help of improvised spades hacked out of driftwood,
And the scooping of narrow, regulated channels

So that quantities of water transferred in cartons
Might be pushed and manoeuvred from one point to the next.
You can never say ants are organised while one ant
Pisses off in quiet serendipity from the ranks,
Or that humans are individual while these nine
All dispose themselves in such unison, and delight
In the antics of brackish sea water and grains of sand
Gone black with the dull consensus of the polities
To crowd out our oceans with mercantile detritus;
And you could even say that a literary eye
Was giving itself unnecessary dilemmas
In pondering whether to organise such data
Into structures of formal sense, when the thing might prove
A sociological question, a case of how
An extended middle-class family runs itself
In nineteen-seventy-eight, as it cheerfully finds
A scheme of elaborate play on a tarnished beach,
The elders pushing their young to be entrepreneurs
And learn a tremendous work-ethic learning to coax
The spillings of obstinate water to the right spot,
. . . I suppose one might let it fade, a small cameo
Of a decorative kind, quiet plastic enjoyments
Going dimmer as the figures merge with the twilight,
And the calls die distantly in the nostalgic dusk
(The parents retiring, the children turning into
Young Eurocrats, or producing some kind of let-down,
And the future arriving with its ancient, heartless,
Recurring prospect of *déjà vu* and *plus ça change*)
– Except that it glows in the mind with a feverish,
Even wilful colour, on the memory's small screen:
The cavorting torsos crazy about their rituals,
The sun blazing uncontradictably, just this once,
On a long terrain of water and sand resplendent
With an unexpected heat-wave; an erratic case
Of forgivable weather in a summer that gave
Not many days to build castles in the open air.

176 *Especially*

To Frank and Rita in Bracknell, greetings,
And greetings especially to those listeners who,
On this weatherless February day at half-past four,
Have risen from first long lovebeds in small warm rooms
To lie again in magenta baths together,
And dabble each other's steaming thighs with suds.

I especially feel
For those who have long-delayed essays on Tennyson to write,
And have switched on their English transistors to discover
Some Third Republic operetta tripping out
On Radio 3, all coquettish plaints
And cavalier manoeuvres, happening out there
In the distance and the past, and so near and true.

May you, especially, recline, as you listen to the voices
Of love made easy and gracious ploys fulfilled,
And renew the heat of the water from time to time
From the tap marked 'Varm' (if you're listening in

Stockholm),
And float the soap in play towards each other's
Crotches, in the softly dropping dark,
And chatter for only a sentence or two of what
Might be, and what might prevent it in a thoughtless world.

Greetings to you then, especially, and here
Is *Das Lied von der Erde*.

177 *Heptonstall February*

Today the moors unclench and clench
On a gift of warmth; the snow
Draws back one softened inch, but frost holds firm.
In our mid-afternoon new ice already
Glints, in the sun's very eye. A camera-eye
Would trace the loosened stream, and stop
On a rigid freeze: where suddenly grey
Spires, that were a waterfall, stab down
At the shrunken torrent.
                                   None of these days
Will release themselves, the land
Not gentle into sympathy. This cold
Is well ignored by those who wait indoors
Inside their coloured windows, watching
The month increase and the land not change:
Let it come to the light and listen.

178 *Near Gun Hill*

Once drawn to promontories where the sea
Is grey and intemperate, with sheer juts
Of rock into rapacious, upheaved waters . . .
At Hartland Point in fog a bursting roar
Blares out on time and space from the lighthouse
And deafens its own echoes; while inland
Merely a sweet haze drapes the sunset fields.
Or at Rhossilli, or the Calf of Man:
A savagery interposes on the path
Of sun- or moonlight laid across that bleak
Table of restlessness, and breaks all thought.
Once drawn to this; and therefore not believing
Any disquiet on one rare windless day
Lying down and gazing on endless sands

On this eastern coast, line above line, and each
A deepening dried yellow to the edge,
With the last line the horizon: all a stave
Still innocent of anything's notation
– And to feel suddenly how the huge chords
Don't dramatise themselves, don't flaunt themselves
In obvious frenzies here, but lie and wait
While the first creature of the swarm climbs slowly
Unsheathing a black wing and tilts one reed.

179 *A Bad Cat Poem*

In the spring of their hope you saw them crouching,
He outside in the sunshine and she inside,
And handling this bad cat back and forth, to and fro
Through the flap. And back through the flap.
They were trying to coax it to work the flap.

That summer the cat was not learning at all,
Though they pushed it persistently, head
First and tail last, towards each other
Through the yielding flap in the humid dark,
She inside, he outside, with fists full of moulted hairs.

And by the autumn still it had not learnt,
While the air was not kindly any more:
The flap on its hinges grated, he outside
Forcing hard the reluctant brute to her inside,
Who received it with aching hands.

It had to be winter next; it would not learn now.
It had never made it once of its own accord:
It had only ever let itself passively
Be jostled to and fro through the grinding hole,
To and fro, back and forth, she inside, he outside,

And both of them getting horribly impatient.

His liquid lunches will not have unhoned
This lean man, upright at the bar
With the minutes of the last executive
In a thick buff wallet, listening precisely
And working through strategies. His brow
Is furrowed with niceties, his craft
Is the unravelment and intertwining
Of clauses in tense agreements. He gives
A week-end course in grievance and recompense,
And Monday, drives via home to all his high
Cabinets of cases, when the telephone
Clangs to the carpet as he stretches out far to a file
On a distant shelf, and listening precisely.
In a city where minds are slabbed with gold,
He builds a sheltering-wall of brick; and how
The commonwealth doth need such justices.

181 *The Leap*

One Xmas in the High Street, the Rotary Tree
On the traffic island by the underground Gentlemen's
Concealed a plenteous amplifier, bawling
The sound of music as if from down below.

Rotarians were shaking boxes for children
Too far away, too heathen, or too poor
To have this kind of Xmas; and two lovers
Looked out upon this scene from where they sat

– On a cushion of white noise which they could not hear –
At the cotton-wool-snow-dotted window of
A little formica restaurant, threading hands
And picking at green salads between interlacements.

That deep hum of noise from the near deep freeze
Lulled all the sounds around them, held them fast
From the clamours of the Xmas street, kept off
This world altogether, more than they would have guessed.

All they could know was a happy avenue
Stretching away in front of them, and on
Into uplands of opportunity; and they thought:
Of all the times, this time we have it right!

– When suddenly a sneaky thermostat
Cut the droning freezer out to the starkest stop;
And with a squirming chill down every back,
The whole room took a leap into a ghastly

Stillness, and vividness. Their hands disjoined,
And to their eyes came nervous, separate smiles,
Much less certain than before: that wicked cold
Went through their empty fingers to their hearts,

And froze out words. So when the shaken room
Relaxed, and as the seething copper urn
Spilled out once more its rasping twists of coffee
Into trays of passive cups, they had this instinct

Of a string having somehow snapped in the distant air
– Until the traffic moved, and the tree again
Stood and ritually glistened, and everyone
Went deaf as usual with the chime of coin.

182 *Holding Hands with Pregnant Women*

Somewhere a bus drives on, on this chilling night
Of dusty April, between its termini,
The conductor winding his destinations
Backwards and forwards as if to obtain some
Renewal of the sense of quest; and these two
            Sit inside it all this time,

Holding hands and not noticing. She repeats,
'You would have wanted this child to be your own?'
And he gives her illusion no denial,
Having loved her enough, long since, to have felt
Exactly such a thing for about nine weeks
            When they met by the bandstand.

But truly he is thinking now, 'How can she
Be ever complete again, ever the same
As the woman of the past, when our pledges
Were engraved in deep letters and in our eyes
When we kissed by the boating-lake in the fog,
            And I could not bear to lose

The hand I capture now in this neutral way
Which *she* does not grasp?'
                              – But let them travel on.
Give or take a variation of detail,
It could be happening almost anywhere,
Wherever a woman gives a man her news
            And he makes out he is pleased,

Yet not for one moment wants her happiness,
Preferring a slow gathering of regret,
Of self-doubt about her marriage, and a fear
That she may have spoilt her life when, instead, she –
But pregnant today, she feels magnanimous
            Towards all unregenerate

Lovers arrived out of the past, who have lost
Their cutting edge of novelty or nuisance:
Those old, superannuated cavaliers
Who send birthday presents through friends' addresses
Or make phone calls to the office, gentle bores
            Who will always minister

To the last shards of romance, her tiny crave
For a tremor of nostalgia now and then.
There is this sweet island in her consciousness
Where the trees gleam even now with untaken
Fruit from those evenings on the rustic bridges
            Making quips about moorhens,

Having schemes about beds in far-off cities;
And even now, she thinks, he would if he could,
He would pluck it if she let him, and suck, suck:
So he holds her hand, in London or Belgrade,
Allowing these assumptions to have their rein
          – Yet wherever they may be,

He is looking for the sudden prize: the chance
To re-start the process all over again
With another one; at forty or fifty,
To begin a brand-new journey through it all,
All over again (the new girl saying how
          Alien it would be, in

Her married or unmarried state, to even
Dream of bearing children, how she quite intends
To stay sterile for her career, for the sake
Of peace and quiet, or fulfilment through batiks,
While she takes the pill, and smokes, and wonders if
          This Jungian analyst

Can put her together, and whether she should
Consent to be chairperson of her local
Liberal Women's Group). How he longs for it
All to flood back, that poignant high adventure
Of plunging into young women still unsoiled
          By cash and security . . .

He will therefore grip her patronising hand
Rather nominally, on whatever route
They ride today; and will outwardly maintain
A reverence for their past, and try to show
A nostalgia for it out of chivalry,
          As the unborn child begins

To chafe inside her. – And she would not believe
That last night's yearning for the larger size of
Gherkins, in big glossy jars, which you notice
On the counters of downmarket sidestreet pubs,
Was a throwback to their first drink ever, at
          The Hare and Hounds in Catford.

Condemn it as a *fainéant* indulgence;
But nations without it fix their constitutions,
Buy personnel carriers from Western powers,
                    And refine kinetic art.

Having nostalgia is having a proper respect
For small lights receding on a shore, without
Dismissing *all* pioneers who sternly steam off
                    Across the Forward Planner.

Not having it is licensing Zakki and Tobia
To patronise Nik and Germaine for their funny names
In 1998. Is saying, 'Look at these craptious
                    Gears in these merdy old photes!'

When it's not as if the nostalgic were saying
'Revere them in their dignified garments, fragile
In the beautiful black-and-white past; from them
                    We derive all truth.' We are not such fools.

One bad mistake, I agree, is reducing nostalgia
To wanton revivals of old detritus:
Hobbit socks and Whitelaw cardigans need not
                    Come back again in my lifetime;

And one better form of nostalgia is a hatred
Of the arrogance of time ever passing: Adolf Hitler
Drank gallons of weak tea and ate cream cakes,
                    And raved all night about the *future*;

He should have sat with the nostalgic, reminiscing
From evening round to dawn, and when dawn comes
One says, 'Do you remember how we sat last night
                    Indulging our nostalgia? How sweet it was . . .'

Then didn't someone say nostalgia was not
A weakness, but a springboard? From where you stand,
With the warm past cheering you on, you dive away
        Into the coming minutes reassured

That they also will cheer you to recall them.
Don't listen to any injunction to 'Cut adrift,
Forget what you cannot change.' Think long enough
        About anything past, and it improves.

– My horror is of losing all regard for any
Caress, or meal, or music from yesterday. I would never
Willingly let it all go slipping like a splendid
        Orchestra out to sea. My dread

Is of being a forgetful old man at ninety
Hustled onwards, always onwards, turned right off
The dances of his youth (though he rarely danced them)
        And set there, stark upon the shore,

Amidst a rubbish from times-to-come: the trees
Casting polythene leaves, the calendar metric,
And each bit of flotsam swirling round his feet
        Singing, 'Hey! My name's *Tomorrow*! Bite me
                       NOW!'

184   *A View of Sussex*

Our happy road is flanked by russet guards-
Of-honour, for November: tiny leaves
Flit at our wheels in suicidal pairs
As we drive powerfully south. You shake your head
Because you want to rearrange the hair
You won't let anybody see you comb
Except yourself. – And there, see how the lamp
Lights up those gables where the vine has turned
A dry vermilion round the 'Hawk and Prey',

Which flaps and creaks for the wind. We smell of air
As I grip hard on our receptionist's
Black ballpen, and write lies. But further in,
Along the corridors, the mantle of
The central heat comes down, a thrilling hush
Which deepens in our room. We drop our bags
Hard on a bench of wooden slats, we let
The tap drip and the light stay on, we start
Clutching the white stiff sheets to tear them back
As if we were ravening at new bread.

185   At Middleton St George

The buzz of a mechanical game played by working
Two handles, one on each side of a screen
Where you shift around an always-too-late white line
In the effort to stop a blip which flies very fast
Over a small dark firmament, you lose a point
If you don't contrive to intercept it; and gin,
And bubbles rising in the tonic, or clinging
To the side of the glass, expiring hopes:
An aerodrome building, converted not long back
Into a student lounge, with bar and cushions,
Double-glazed against the whining air, but somehow
The room is forced to admit the scream as it pierces
The level land outside, jet engines droning
On their high and undismissible register, dropping
Down fast to this haven of their firmament,
A sound striking suddenly through, as when you feel water
Reach inside a soaped ear.
                                    The runways were laid down
For a war predating mechanical games you can play

On buzzing screens, but resulting in radar,
And out across the acres of grass and tarmac
Stand air-force buildings of one and two storeys
Converted into a college for several hundred,
Made over into bedsits and lecture-rooms and that
Barrack is the library, with long open aisles
Of volumes for learning about learning.

                      Sitting there
You can try intercepting an idea before it flicks past
(Without working a handle) but not for long now:
The engines will soon inherit the place again, the ideas
Expire, like all hopeful bubbles. For thirteen years
You could eat in the echoing refectory, run
A moderate lap on the games floor laid down inside
The hangar; but an unlettered wind wipes all
This land quite clean of learning, the students leave,
The last ministrants see them out.

                      Eight years ago,
Ruth furrowed in that index for critical assistance
With the novels of D.H.Lawrence, and walked along
To a corner where they went to each other's arms
And her shoulder, for a moment, unbalanced a small row
Of volumes at 823.LAWR. And eight years ago,
They all fell back into place, in perfect order,
As he let Ruth go, not to be kissed again ever
By him, and watched her recede down the heartless
Perspective of the grass, farther off and farther still,
And go in for her Finals.

                  The ceiling of chandeliers
Above our student lounge makes a carapace against
The huge skies of this region, but the crude lid-lifters
Will prise it away, and we shall shiver
From more than nostalgia, and then relinquish it
To the fractured sky over the runways, allow
The Lawrence files to break open at their spines, pages
Flutter away into the slipstreams and vanish
In a distance which does not read. The flying blips
Fled past too fast, we were always too late.

                                        That ivy,
Which grew untrained up the wall of the Admin. block,
Rattles red against the brickwork, the colour it turned to
And stayed throughout last winter; a louder sound
Than any inside, where the rooms now scream with silence;
And there's the last bubble faintly expiring in
Our tonic water, like a lamp of Europe.
                                   Oh, but now
There is suddenly a triumphant jumping of feet
On the carpet up by the screen, because someone
Has deflected his final blip, and won! What a pity
It's a game and not real . . . One says about the real,
There are too many evils to prevent, or even
Notice them all, as you strive to work the hopeless
Handles you are offered, like using sardine-tin keys
For programming computers.
                             There was Ruth here once,
And the fall of her hair across the shaken spines
Of the Lawrence critics, and her lover's spine tilting
Towards her at 823.LAWR. He was one who read,
Like most of us, not wisely but too late,
And what should he have learnt?
                                  And what have I?
–Hardly much more than one negative consolation:
There are too many evils, they race too fast, you lose
Much more than a point if you don't contrive to intercept them.

1980s

At first it looked as if the horse
    Came riderless, out of the green
Woods in the dropping night; and then
    We knew what we had really seen
Was Cheryl, draped with a green coat
    To match the dark and deepening shade
And make the white horse seem as if
    It strode alone across the glade.
– And had we stopped our borrowed car
    Ten yards uphill or ten yards down,
Or left its headlights on and caused
    Cheryl to switch her dazzled frown
And fix it on the trees that day,
    Not seeing us with fingers tight-
ly laced together on the gear-
    Stick knob – it might have been all right.
Instead, we chose the very point
    Where Cheryl (who had been advised
To give up riding for her health)
    Chose to emerge, and thus surprised
The two of us parked near the Mill,
    Facing the sunset. First she stared
At Polly, then she froze at me
    – My theory is she was prepared
To speak to us, then changed her mind –
    Firefly was not prepared to wait
On the last hundred yards of his
    Last outing—it was getting late,
So Cheryl did not rein him in,
    But let him stride on up the track
(And having summed up what she saw,
    Saw little point in looking back.)
And there were many interests
    A Cheryl of this life might find
In church, or bridge, or marquetry,
    To occupy an active mind;

And various were the causes which
    Resourceful Cheryl might have made
Her own: opposing the closed shop,
    Collecting old gold teeth in aid
Of pensioners or hospitals
    Or sewage systems, wearing a tray
Of flags to help the unemployed
    In the best nineteen-eighties way;
But Cheryl chose to ride instead,
    And lurking fate chose equally
To have her leave the twilight wood
    At just the point where she would see.
And so we knew that Cheryl knew
    About our meetings by the Mill,
And this was worse for being on
    A day she told us she was ill,
And now there were no lies to spin,
    And no excuses to invent,
As Cheryl had our number, and
    The shape of things was different.

187   *Inheritors*

The snow is at the same time as the owl;
When it drops down to the sill, the wings close,

First question: *Why should the owl*
Fly down each night to peer at our painted room?

Softly the snow-dots tumble from its back
As it stands on still claws and looks in,

Second question: *Why does the owl*
Stare in so long at our wine and velvet chairs?

Away from its nest, old feathers, suspicious gaze,
Away if you walk near the window, but always back,

Third question: *If one of us has summoned it,*
Which?

— And so we sit, four men in a shared house,
In a particularly scarlet room,
Not easy as we snow down cards, four
After four on the shining table-top;

Not easy as our fingers claw them in;

Wondering what is meant by these visits
From two old interested eyes, not easy
Wondering also which of us might know.

188   *You'll See*

They all talked about growing into,
Growing into, growing into.
They said: You will grow into it.

— But it isn't mine,
And it's not for me.
— You will grow into it,
You'll see!

— But it hangs down below my knee,
It is too long for me.
— Oh it will fit you soon,
It will fit you splendidly.

— But I will sulk, and I will say
It is too long, it is no use,
No! I will sulk, and struggle,
And refuse!

– You will grow into it,
And love it,
And besides, we decided
You should have it.

No! – But wait –
Wait a moment . . . Do I see
It growing shorter at the knee?
Is it shrinking gradually?
Is it getting shorter?
Is it getting tighter?
Not loose and straggly,
Not long and baggy,
But neater and brighter,
Comfortable?

Oh now I *do* like it,
Oh now I'll go to the mirror and see
How wonderful it looks on me,
Yes – there – it's ideal!
Yes, its appeal
Will be universal,
And now I curse all
Those impulses which muttered 'Refuse!'
It's really beautiful after all,
I'll wear it today, next week, next year
– No one is going to interfere,
I'll wear it as long as I choose.

And then, much later, when it wears,
And it's ready for dumping under the stairs
When it doesn't actually really fit me
Any longer, then *I'll* pass it down,
When it doesn't fit me,
And then they'll have it,
They'll *have* to have it,
They'll have to love it,
They'll see, they'll see.

They'll have to grow into it like me!

Look how faded and worn the sun is, like old linen.
But it lights my neat young grandfather brightly
To the door of the little contraceptive shop;

Where his fancy has engaged with the yellowed sets
Of enveloped possibilities, their very formal
Old typography. Into an even further faded

Interior, he allows, as he pushes at the door,
An allocation of the ancient light
Discreetly, and vanishes from the lens, which holds

The window and the sunblinds only so long
As some graininess of image lets it seem
That dust is gathering on both shop and street

Even as I watch. This cuts to an unmade avenue,
A house, a sepia bedroom where high pots
Of flowering rubber plants, broad Chinese screens,

And beads low at a neckline entertain,
By being my grandmother's obviously, hopes
That I have been watching this film myself,

Not some interloping shadow, standing at
That young man's shoulder, a black care
Sitting behind the horseplay, about to expose it,

Like his near-fatal typhoid at twenty-three.

Well, once we told people's fortunes, but now
We sit in our robes and fish from the pier,
We fish from the pier; though they call to us
That the sea receded many a year
Ago, on our little camp stools we sit
And fling out our hooks at low green land where
Children walk by with their dogs through the grass,
And the slight summer breeze makes waves in it.

Well, we are wise and we are ready, when
The dyke they have built to hold back the brute
Sea shatters in the distance, for a full
Rampaging day there will then come waves not
Consisting of grass; and in pain and blood,
The children and dogs will be crying out
– And with our lines and hooks and prayers, we will
Fish from the pier in the horrible flood.

191   *Watershed*

I detected this change in the ways of my friends:
They had suddenly gone in for a decent shame
In their lunch-time conversations; no longer were they
Boasting of all their adulteries and grand lies.

Their talk had become decidedly more discreet.
They did not want to confess, and seek reassurance.
They did not stub out their cigarettes half way
And stumble out to make illicit phone calls,

And I said: This is really very seemly,
There are some of us who have found some strength at last,
This restaurant at lunch-time is no longer
A vista of private misery, a place

Where novice waiters are brought in to learn
How to come and steal away our untouched plates
With an unseen patience. And I thought it good
That my friends should have acquired some self-control.

But then, one day as the two of us were sitting
With nothing to say, and the band filled in
Our silence with its genteel sympathies,
I felt sad about all this; and began to search

The back of my mind to drag out some anecdote
Of hazard and betrayal to revive those dear
Dead days . . . And I found that I did not have one.
Then I saw that your hand, which I recalled would once

Have crawled to mine for comforting across
Whole Sohos of wine-stained tablecloths,
Had apparently forgotten my hand was there,
And was checking the bill, which we were halving,

As were all the other hands on all the other
Tables across the endless dry-eyed room;
Above which stood a clock with its own hand
Shifting neutrally one second on towards five past two.

192 *Dialogue of the Striving Soul
and the Deprecating Self*

>   Soul: I release the worn black handle,
>   And slap the last ball straight up
>   To the top of the frame; where
>   It pauses long enough, just,
>   To shape the whole arcade into
>   A tiny silver picture before
>   It turns at last, and wanders
>   Derisively down and across

Not hitting any exciting coils
Not bouncing any further red
Numerals into lights increasing
Speed missing all connections
Dropping finally back into
Its pit.
          My little score
Shines out for one brief moment, and then goes dark.

Self: Ah, soul! You ought to realise how
      You did not remotely deserve
      Those encouraging lights and that
      Working handle when others
      Were fretting in long queues to get
      No turn in the end, or discovered
      That the chrome slit swallowed
      All their money and sent them down
      No balls at all, while the button
      Refused to return their coins. And of course,
      Over there all the time the real boys,
      With huge muscles and girls to praise them,
      And deep uproarious voices,
      Were playing the real game . . .
                          And don't think they
      Couldn't see you trying quietly to tilt the machine.

193 *Stepping Out*

Stepping out from under mother's
Protection at five or fifty,
Up the ever-so-nasty wet
Miles of tarmac to the moor,
Bold to cross it though his short
Legs, he saw, were trembling,
He arrived at the wind-worsted heather

Out of reach of her voice, whether
Raised in anger or muted
In consolation. These were forbidden
Tracts, so remote from mother's suburb,
And what wonderful courage this was!

To have even started out was
Appalling audacity, loading
His belongings without her help,
Taking boots, map and compass
And creeping out to the door . . .
Could this truly be himself?
And could this invincible dawn be
Raining, as he set off, when she
Had predicted a sunny day with her?
It scared him. It soothed him knowing
How surely he would be creeping back
When the day was over.

And he could not tell if he might
Be prouder of having defied
Mother's warnings, or of guessing
How deeply he would defer again
To her, in the end . . . Down there below,
The voices of the crowd cried amazement
That mother's own particular
Weakling had gone so far;
And the little voice here at his side
Said the venturing out in dread
And the going back from fear
Were both attributable to her.

A guilty tremor in the chime of six
From his dishevelled mantelpiece . . . She waits
For the plaint of the express along the cutting,
Which she guesses the wind will let her hear,
Then she rises, in a calm of strict obedience,
And walks off obediently to be back,
Securely seated in her drawing-room,
As the doors of the carriages gape and slam.

– Though one day the train has left, she is running
And scarcely home before her lawyer husband
Is entering and handing his hat naively
To the discreet old fellow in the hall.
Catching her breath, she comes in from the garden
As if from the garden and nowhere else,
Dividing the curtains no more than her hair
Would be slightly rearranged by an innocent breeze.

– And later still, one day the whistle-call
Dies out, she hears it, over the summer fields,
And she does not move at all. She stands here still,
Though the train is already some way on,
And allocating other destinies.
The lawyer is destined to the empty house.
Her hair is neat. She smiles for the man in this room.
He stares at his prize incredulous and afraid.

195 *A Statue of Innocence*

or

Geological Time in the Department

(for John Betjeman)

Miss Frith was put on processing; that glue
And all those labels. Not seven months there,
And Mr Mortimer, who always said
'Miss Frith' and never 'Gill' or 'Gillian',
Right through the informal nineteen-sixties,
Rested one day his two hands on her hips
As she sat cross-leggéd on the high stool
At the labelling desk. She did not squirm,
She did not put the labels down; to be
A statue of innocence was her way
Of making Mr Mortimer redeem
His fingers, which (to be fair) he had not
Spread out all that widely.

                      After ten months,
Miss Frith was briefly told by Miss Duveen
How Mr Langley, in the previous year,
Had twice put his arm round her shoulders in
The Lower Stack Room. No, it had not been
A question of her having felt some need
Of comforting, or of her wanting help
With the box-files; he had just come and put
His arm around her, and had no excuse
– An honesty for which he would obtain
A tick in the Eternal Register.

Five months went by. Then, Mr Mortimer
Suddenly kissed Miss Frith, full on the lips,
On the little-used back staircase between
The Processing Room and the Staff Canteen.

Five months! So things were speeding up. But times
Were frantic, what with the renovations,
And he never did anything else. All
Over the building lay the dusty planks,
The stepladders and dust-sheets, brought by bald
And jocular young white-coated builders,
Who painted and sang to small transistors.
They were apt to appear round any corner;
One could not really use that staircase now.

Miss Frith occasionally wondered what
Inscrutable inertia it was that kept
The silent Mr Langley three short yards
Away from her, at his metal table,
Through so many busy and humid days
Spent loathing the central heating. Of course,
She would not have welcomed an intrusion;
But she would have looked for *something*. 'In time,
Even the rocks,' she read, 'will change their shape.'

She doubted it. One day in May, Miss Frith
Lifted her eyes from all the labels on
The labelling desk, and put down her brush,
And observed that the dust in the still air
Was thinner than it had been. It was quiet,
The builders gone and the renovations
Finished till the next time. Now, suddenly,
With eyes less prone to notice than to gaze
(With dull eyes pleading for the world to change)
She saw that the traffic down there in the street,
Passing and crossing, on through day and dark
And never ceasing, was re-organized
Into an irreversible One Way.

Rain, said Nanny, Rain is to test our courage,
Dirt is to test our cleanliness,
Hunger our patience,
And night is to test our fear of darkness.
But rain is to test our courage.

That was because it rained all the time very hard
Where we lived as children,
In the house with the nineteen rooms of forbidden books
(To test how we could conquer the thirst to read)
And a few permitted books in the sitting rooms,
But Nanny in a book-lined room we might never enter,
In a turret above the lawn where the croquet hoops
Were feet deep in water for very much of the time.

But Courage, said Nanny, wellingtons on,
Backs up, chins up, and best foot forward
In a long line, holding tightly on to each other
– Out!

So the small but courageous band of us
Paddled hand-in-hand onwards,
Nanny first, me second,
Then the third and fourth, diminishing in size
To the very smallest who came infallibly last,
Head just above water.

And as we sadly struggled, the small cold hand
Of my youngest brother
Slipped out of the grasp of the one next above him in age.
And when that next one tired, her hand
Released the fingers of the sibling senior to her,
And the line fell gradually apart,
Leaving me
Waving frantically after Nanny, who was far ahead
And had almost disappeared.

But *Courage!*

The call of Nanny rang distantly over
The widening waters in the dark,
And returned in echoes from the other shore.
The waterfowl answered in imitation and unison
To comfort each other

And Nanny's cry merged into theirs,
Growing fainter and fainter in the rain until
It became at last an everyday sound you hear
And think little about for very much of the time.

197   *The Pool*

To carry daylight to the pool I walk
Myself in that direction, throwing off
Its veil of grey with my eyes, hurling back
Tall hillsides with each step, causing enough
Space on it for the sky. But as the sky
Glides up and stops in front of me, I stop
And look – Somehow my head is only
A blur itself on the water's edge, my face
Is darkened by the half-light of this place
. . . You could remove me just as easily.

I could change nature with no greater power
Than a short walk, and a switching of my gaze;
But I see now that my shape is nothing more
Than a shadow on this world, and its brief day dies.
I go back to a room where there is room
For just a mirror – another mirror
In which I make no difference. This one is deep,
And in it, stones and earth will not retreat
For movements of the head, or of the feet.
Nothing can alter there. And nothing keep.

236

They would call me soon. And still I stood
At some window on the cold side of the house,
Somewhere between this and non-existence,
Letting the evening rotate towards me,
Fixing my gaze on nothing at all.

All the life in the place had left suddenly,
And gone out to the terrace. But I stayed one
With the objects in this room, in their graveyard poise
Of dresser, bed, and vase. Everything seemed
Too dull to be worth a judgement, first or last,

And too dead to be raised by voices; it felt
Too late already. If they had sent up
From down below to fetch me, *Come on, we're waiting!*
They would have found only a shape you could not
Prise out from the furniture and the shadows.

– So I quite surprised myself when I started
Running easily down stairs, round corners, and out
Through a door into the sun. And can't explain
The laughter, the groans of welcome, the shuffling up,
Or my head and shoulders in the photograph.

199   *Jogger*

The man on the liniment bottle is very young.
He is gaining rapid relief from muscular pains
Which must have set in early. I am rigorous
Like him, I know I am . . . But I do think,
Would my wrists ache if I rubbed my heavy legs
In the rigorous way required? Would I then need
To rub each rigorous wrist? And if so, how?

So how dignified, I think, that old Einstein
On the cough-drop tin, who stands up tall and straight,
And shakes his great grey sneezing head into
A starch-white handkerchief, trimly tucked
In a dignified black pocket. How easy,
Only to have to stretch one dignified
Hand to a tin for one all-solving jube!

200 *Doorway*

Where it stood by the roadside, the frame for a view,
It made the step from one weed-patch to the next
A metaphor. If I chose to walk across
This threshold to a mansion never built,
Could I manage to come back? Having left the road
To stroll into the fields, I saw this lintel
Presenting its challenge. And what it said was, *Walk*

Through this door, you are going to walk through,
After which you will not be the same. I had thought,
Was I always on a journey to that place?
– And now, was I always travelling to where
I am to-night, by a fire toning down to grey
Its image in those glasses, beside the girl
Asleep in the opposite chair? To such a stop?

To-night is six months onwards from that voice
Which said, *You have reached a stage where you must walk through,*
And not expect to return to what you were.
I am here because I turned back from that view,
Shaking my head and smiling, walking on
To where this girl smiles, in apparent sleep,
And stretches. What she does first when she wakes

Is pick the glasses up, they suddenly
Shine scarlet from the curtains. *What were you thinking?*
She says, as she goes past. I shake my head,
And smile, watching the fire. She goes on past
Its dying coil, then I realise she has stopped
And turned at the doorway behind me, tilting
The glasses in her hand. And has said, *Walk through.*